Contribution to (

Praise for this book

'Evaluation practitioners will find this book to be an extremely valuable resource. The book is easy to use and sets out a clear step-by-step approach for assessing multiple agency interventions at the community level.'

Scott Green, Chief of Evaluation, Office for the Co-ordination
of Humanitarian Affairs (OCHA)

'The expectations for humanitarian and development workers are increasingly more professionalized. Many participate in evaluations without extensive training or academic background. This clear, concise book adds a useful, practical method to our arsenal of evaluation tools and includes step-by-step information that will be very accessible to field staff.'

Anne Castleton, PhD, Director of Disaster Risk Reduction,
Strategic Response and Global Emergencies, Mercy Corps

'The humanitarian sector has grappled for some time to develop a sound methodology for assessing the impact of interventions where no counterfactual can be identified and no baseline following a disaster exists. *Contribution to Change* provides a clear step-by-step guide and robust methodology for assessing an agency's interventions by disaster-affected people themselves. This book will be a valuable addition to any evaluator's library.'

Annie Devonport, Head of Programmes and Accountability,
Disasters Emergency Committee

'I am happy to see another ECB publication providing straightforward guidelines for complex situations, with a plain English, common-sense approach to assessing contributions to disaster recovery. Too often the complexity of the context is only matched by the complexity and length of the guidance, and the tendency is to promote imported best practice rather than a locally appropriate "best fit". In this case the authors have avoided those traps.'

Chris Roche, author of Impact Assessment in Development Organisations,
Associate Professor and Chair in International Development,
La Trobe University, Australia

'The clarity offered in *Contribution to Change* will mean that the methodology can actually be applied and owned by time-short field practitioners.'

Moira Reddick, Coordinator, Nepal Risk Reduction Consortium

'This very clear and concise book, written by authors with decades of experience among them, equips practitioners with the tools needed to improve the quality of evaluation in post-disaster response – a critical area that the humanitarian community has been weak in for too long.'

David Sanderson, Visiting Professor of Urban Planning and Design,
Graduate School of Design, Harvard University

Contribution to Change

An approach to evaluating the role of intervention in disaster recovery

Roger Few, Daniel McAvoy, Marcela Tarazona
and Vivien Margaret Walden

PRACTICAL ACTION
Publishing

Published by Practical Action Publishing Ltd in association with Oxfam GB

Practical Action Publishing Ltd
The Schumacher Centre, Bourton on Dunsmore, Rugby
Warwickshire CV23 9QZ, UK
www.practicalactionpublishing.org

Oxfam GB
Oxfam House, John Smith Drive
Oxford OX4 2JY, UK

ISBN 978-1-85339-811-7 Hardback
ISBN 978-1-85339-812-4 Paperback
ISBN 978-1-78044-811-4 Library Ebook
ISBN 978-1-78044-487-1 Ebook

Book DOI: http://dx.doi.org/10.3362/9781780448114

Few, R., McAvoy, D., Tarazona, M. and Walden, V.M. (2014) *Contribution to Change: An Approach to Evaluating the Role of Intervention in Disaster Recovery*, Rugby, UK: Practical Action Publishing and Oxford: Oxfam GB.

Since 1974, Practical Action Publishing has published and disseminated books and information in support of international development work throughout the world. Practical Action Publishing is a trading name of Practical Action Publishing Ltd (Company Reg. No. 1159018), the wholly owned publishing company of Practical Action. Practical Action Publishing trades only in support of its parent charity objectives and any profits are covenanted back to Practical Action (Charity Reg. No. 247257, Group VAT Reg. No. 880 9924 76).

Oxfam is a registered charity in England and Wales (No. 202918) and Scotland (SCO 039042). Oxfam GB is a member of Oxfam International.

The information in this publication is correct at the time of going to press.

Cover photo: Jane Beesley/Oxfam
Cover design by Mercer Design
Typeset by Bookcraft Ltd, Stroud, Gloucestershire
Printed by Berforts Information Press

MIX
Paper from
responsible sources
FSC® C013262

Contents

http://dx.doi.org/10.3362/9781780448114.000

Notes on the authors

Roger Few

Dr Few is currently a Senior Research Fellow in the School of International Development at the University of East Anglia. His research focuses on vulnerability, response, and adaptation to natural hazards and climate change, and he has led a series of applied research projects relating to disaster management and disaster risk reduction. Dr Few has extensive research experience in many countries including Bangladesh, Belize, Cameroon, Ecuador, Guatemala, India, Mexico, Rwanda, Sri Lanka, Tanzania, Uganda, and Vietnam, and has published widely. In addition, he worked for several years as a freelance journalist, author, and editor.

Daniel McAvoy

Mr McAvoy is currently a Senior Lecturer at the University of East Anglia in the School of International Development. He previously worked within the non-government (CARE International) and government (AusAID) sectors for 15 years with a focus on working on (or in) countries experiencing conflict and/or humanitarian crisis. His humanitarian field experience includes working in complex emergencies and disasters in Iraq, Kosovo, Macedonia, Solomon Islands, and Aceh and Jogjakarta in Indonesia. He has also led evaluations of disaster responses. His current research examines the effects and impacts of international state-building interventions with a focus on Solomon Islands.

Marcela Tarazona

Dr Tarazona, Senior Consultant at Oxford Policy Management (OPM), is an environmental economist with more than 13 years of academic and consultancy experience. Her work focuses on issues related to disaster risk management, climate change, monitoring and evaluation (M&E), risk, and experimental economics. Marcela is well published and has worked in numerous countries, including Bangladesh, Bolivia, Colombia, Costa Rica, Ethiopia, Indonesia, India, Mexico, Nigeria, and Vietnam. She holds a PhD and an MA in Environmental Economics from Toulouse School of Economics, and is currently a Senior Research Associate at the School of International Development, University of East Anglia.

Vivien Margaret Walden

Dr Walden is currently the Global Humanitarian Monitoring, Evaluation, and Learning Adviser for Oxfam, based in Oxford. Previously she has worked in both development and humanitarian programmes in numerous countries around the world, including Cambodia, Ethiopia, Malawi, Tanzania and Timor-Leste, as well as being part of the response team in major catastrophes such as the 2004 tsunami. She holds a PhD in Evaluation from the University of Manchester and has contributed to sector learning through published papers and conference presentations.

Foreword

As the humanitarian system continues to grow, donors and agencies alike need an accurate picture of what kind of changes, both positive and negative, are brought about by post-disaster interventions. Everyone agrees about how important this is, but measuring change is easier said than done, and past experiences have thrown up many challenges. This new guide is both timely and useful as it recognizes the constraints and difficulties, presenting a practical and pragmatic approach to assessing change.

The guide is based on two key themes that have recently received increasing attention from both evaluation researchers and practitioners. The first is that changes at the household level result from an interplay of various factors over and above single interventions. Change is not a linear process based solely on programme outputs, but rather the result of a unique coming together of different forces and influences that combine in different ways depending on context. The second theme is about understanding and assessing change through the lens of individual households and communities by capturing shifts in their lives and livelihoods. This means that an understanding of change, positive or negative, is not externally constructed but directly related to personal experiences.

Taking these two key themes as a starting point, the guide presents a broad approach to assessing change, allowing for a more contextual and realistic appraisal of aid which is likely to be very popular with evaluators and managers alike.

Of course, this approach is not a panacea and all undertakings of this nature are going to be challenging. The guide recognizes this, and its utility is strengthened as it has been developed and tested in the field and takes account of the needs of practitioners. The guide also makes an important contribution to filling a gap in evaluation guidance by broadening the range of existing evaluation concepts, methods, and approaches. In this way, it represents a valuable complement to the ALNAP guide to evaluating humanitarian assistance.

I am sure that this guide will make an important contribution to improving both the practice of assessing change and the quality of humanitarian evaluation overall.

John Mitchell
Director, Active Learning Network for Accountability and Performance in
Humanitarian Action (ALNAP)

Acknowledgements

The authors would like to thank the following people: Loretta Ishida (CRS), Sophie Martin-Simpson (Save the Children), Driss Moumane (CRS), Hannah Reichardt (Save the Children), Kevin Savage (World Vision International), and Andrea Stewart (ECB) for being on the steering committee; Juan Carlos Arita (Oxfam), Richard Cobb (Merlin), Oliver Eleeza (CARE), Christine Gaignebet (Oxfam), Jamo Huddle (World Vision), Paul Knox Clarke (ALNAP), John Lakeman (CARE), and Christele Morel (Oxfam) for being on the editorial committee; Federica Chiappe (OPM) for assisting with the Sri Lanka field test; Laure Anquez (Oxfam), Catherine Gould (Oxfam), Katharine Trott (UEA), and Karen Parsons (UEA) for logistical and financial management support; Juan Manuel Girón Durini (CONSERVA), Dana Paz (CONSERVA), and David Arrivillaga (SHARE) for support during the Guatemala field test; Kalinga Tudor Silva (University of Peradeniya), Anusha Fernando, Vickneswaran Gunanayakam, and Kanesh Suresh (all Eastern University of Sri Lanka) for support during the Sri Lanka field test; Aparna John (OPM) and Tom Newton-Lewis (OPM) for support during the India field test; and Paul Joicey, Mylvaganam Yogeswaran, and the Oxfam team in Batticaloa and Colombo for logistical support. Finally, a big thank you to all the community members and fieldworkers who took part in the interviews and discussion groups in the three countries.

Introduction

Why choose this method?

Evaluating the effectiveness of post-disaster interventions is an important but challenging task. Practitioners and donors alike have a shared interest in being able to assess the outcomes and impact of projects and donated funds for recovery, rehabilitation, and reconstruction. However, there has been wide acknowledgement of the difficulties in assessing the benefits of interventions, and there is a need for guidance to assist agencies in undertaking evaluations that are robust but affordable.

This guide aims to provide one reliable and practical method for identifying the contribution to change achieved by external interventions in the recovery period following disasters.

The approach presented here draws from and builds on valuable work by a range of authors – among them Catley et al. (2008), Proudlock et al. (2009), Roche (2010) and Stern et al. (2012). These and other resources are listed in Annex 2.

What is it for?

The purpose of the Contribution to Change approach is to identify how important and effective interventions have been in promoting people's recovery.

It does so by assessing:

- the changes over time in people's lives, with a focus on the extent to which their resources, livelihoods, and well-being have recovered and/or strengthened since the disaster;

- the role that interventions appear to have played in that recovery process.

These are not easy assessments to make. They require careful analysis using different sources of data, but ultimately judgements have to be made on the basis of the evidence available. The more detailed the data collection can be, the more strongly we can make these judgements. However, the design of this methodology is intended to lead to robust conclusions even if the resources for data collection are quite limited. The idea is to provide a methodology that can be readily taken up and adapted for use in the field (see Box 1).

How does it differ?

Existing impact evaluations often focus on outputs achieved or on qualitative assessments of the assistance received by members of affected populations. They tend not to look at the contribution of interventions towards the overall process of recovery.

Also, the context of disaster intervention is complex and changing; there are many diverse actors involved. The work of international agencies cannot always be readily distinguished on the ground from the work of domestic governments and non-governmental agencies. Most importantly, the coping mechanisms and the efforts of community members, their friends and families, and small community-based groups have not been sufficiently acknowledged. The contribution question acknowledges that each agency may play a part in bringing about changes to people's lives, but that there are many factors, including the actions of the affected population themselves, that together determine these outcomes.

There is an increasing call for contribution-based evaluations. However, it is important that measuring change does not become an end in itself but leads ultimately to improving the lives of those affected by the disaster. One key advantage of the approach described here is that, by rooting the analysis in the wider context of people's recovery, it encourages agencies to reflect on the relative impact and consequences of interventions. Ultimately, this should lead to organizational learning and better practice.

Box 1 Why a simple but reliable methodology is required

As the reported number of people affected by disasters has risen through recent decades, so the expectations placed on responding agencies by donors, the public, and affected populations have also increased. This includes a demand that agencies provide evidence of the impact of post-disaster interventions. However, for most agencies there are practical limitations on the extent to which 'gold standard' methods for impact evaluation can be applied.

Resources

Impact evaluations need to be based on a realistic availability of resources, both financial and human. There have been some large-scale household surveys looking at predisaster data and tracking changes over time; examples of these include longitudinal surveys applied after the Indian Ocean tsunami of 2004 and the Pakistan earthquake of 2005 (Buttenheim, 2009). However, the rigour and expense of these longitudinal studies exceed what most agencies can afford in the way of evaluation.

Control groups

The use of control or comparison groups raises costs and poses additional issues. The logical control groups would be disaster-affected communities that do not receive assistance, but working with such groups in post-disaster situations without providing assistance raises ethical concerns. It may also be difficult to identify genuinely comparable communities.

Baseline/endline

Although the more accepted method for measuring the impact of interventions is to have a baseline/endline assessment (i.e. before and after the intervention), in humanitarian programmes it is often difficult for agencies to carry out a baseline early enough to be able to do a comparison. Life-saving and emergency measures take precedence over data collection in the early stages after the onset of a disaster. Traumatized communities may not wish to participate in surveys and discussion groups that do not appear to bring any immediate relief to their situation. Pre-emergency data may be available from other sources, such as government national household surveys or other agency data. However, it may be difficult for agency staff to extrapolate the information needed for their particular target group or the quality may be such that it is not considered useful.

Which types of post-disaster situation is it used for?

The Contribution to Change methodology is designed mainly to be used in the situation following rapid-onset natural hazards such as flash floods, storms, landslides, earthquakes, tsunamis and volcanic eruptions.

However, there is potential for the method to be modified and applied to slow-onset natural hazards such as drought (see the note in Part One, Figure 3).

The approach is normally used in situations where there has been external intervention (see Box 2) intended to foster people's recovery in the medium term. These interventions may be in any sector or across different sectors. It is *not* designed to assess the effectiveness of immediate life-saving or short-term emergency relief (see Table 1).

The approach is normally applied in communities of people who have continued to reside in the same sites since the disaster, and are looking to restore or improve their lives and livelihoods in the recovery period. It can be applied or modified for situations in which there has been temporary displacement following disasters, but we do not recommend the approach for situations of ongoing displacement (see Annex 3 for further details on situations of displacement).

The approach can also be used for situations in which disaster risk-reduction efforts have been under way to reduce future vulnerability to hazards.

The methodology is intended to be flexible. It can be applied to small- or large-scale disasters, to specific communities or across regions receiving aid programmes.

Box 2 What does 'intervention' mean in this approach?

The term 'intervention' is used in a general sense in this guide. It refers to post-disaster responses in affected communities undertaken by external organizations (i.e. actions not taken by the community themselves, but by international, national, or sub-national organizations, including governments). In most situations the method will be used in the context of a range of actions, in which case the term 'intervention' refers to the collective activities of different aid programmes rather than the efforts of one agency. This is because the methodology is designed to gather information about how people's lives have been shaped since the disaster, which leads to a broad view of change rather than a focus on the efforts of one particular agency. However, it is also acknowledged that, at times, evaluation of a single agency's actions may be applicable.

Change for whom?

The design of the evaluation depends a great deal on the question of whose change the evaluators are trying to assess. Is it change for the community in general or change for the recipients of the intervention, or both?

In this guide, the working assumption is that the evaluators are interested in establishing the pattern of recovery in affected communities and the contribution of interventions to that change. This means that recovery processes across the community are important – within particular themes or sectors of interest, such as housing, water supplies, or agricultural livelihood support, as well as recovery in general (across sectors).

It may also be important to understand specifically what has happened for a narrower group of direct beneficiaries of interventions. This may especially be the case if interventions are very small-scale (e.g. applying to one section of a village) or socially targeted (e.g. to older people or fishing families). Annex 4 indicates how the methodology can be modified to place a focus on beneficiaries. However, it is important to note that the divide between beneficiaries and the wider community may in any case not be discrete – interventions may be targeted to certain groups but still have positive effects and negative (unintended) consequences for the wider community.

When should this evaluation be undertaken?

The method is designed to be used within 6 to 12 months of the occurrence of a disaster. A period longer than this will present difficulties in terms of retrospective data collection because of limits on the reliability with which people can recall details of their livelihood changes. (However, this period can be longer if it is possible to undertake an initial phase of data collection shortly after the emergency period, followed by a subsequent phase.)

Who should undertake the evaluation?

Because of its wide-ranging approach in terms of assessing changes across the various actions undertaken in a recovery situation, this methodology is particularly appropriate for joint evaluation exercises between agencies. An Active Learning Network for Accountability and Performance in Humanitarian Action (ALNAP) review suggests that the 'future of humanitarian impact assessment lies in linking different partners across the sector' (Proudlock et al., 2009, p. 74). This guide proposes that multi-agency evaluations can save on resources, will encourage the use of contribution, and will encourage learning. However, the methodology can be adopted by a single agency.

Field staff may be able to undertake the evaluation but they do need a good level of knowledge and skills in research methods. A certain understanding of techniques such as sampling and selection, compiling questionnaires, and working with qualitative data is necessary. Analytical skills in the use of quantitative and qualitative data are key to the success of the method. The authors suggest that in many cases it may be appropriate to commission a third party to carry out the evaluation – especially for an evaluation jointly commissioned by more than one agency (see Part One, 'Planning and management').

Table 1   Uses and limitations of the Contribution to Change approach

WHAT IT IS DESIGNED FOR	Rapid-onset disasters from natural hazards
	Assessing medium-term recovery
	Working with communities that are not (currently) displaced
	Evaluating contribution
	Looking at the contribution to recovery in general
WHAT IT IS NOT DESIGNED FOR	Conflict and complex disasters
	Assessing emergency response and relief
	Working with long-term displaced communities
	Evaluating attribution
	Focusing on specific outputs
	Evaluating efficiency, value for money and sustainability (and other 'process' evaluations)
IT CAN ALSO BE ADAPTED TO ADDRESS	Slow-onset natural hazards
	Disaster risk-reduction activity
	Equity in interventions

The guide and how to use it

The guide is divided into three parts. Part One presents and explains the key components of the approach, Part Two guides the reader through the data collection method, and Part Three presents in detail how the data should be analysed and reported.

It is essential that those using the approach read carefully through all of these parts. A thorough understanding of the approach is required before detailed design of the evaluation can take place. Essential guidelines are provided for a series of 11 steps that need to be undertaken, from preliminary studies to reporting. Suggestions for further reading and information sources are provided for readers to find more generic guidance, especially on themes such as fieldwork management, sampling, data collection instruments and statistical analysis. However, the guide does not provide a blueprint design with pre-prepared question sheets and surveys, because it is essential that the method used in the field is tailored to the circumstances and contexts of the case in question.

Annex 2 compiles details of other resource material that may be useful when designing and undertaking the Contribution to Change evaluation.

The methodology presented in this guide was developed following three pilot studies in India, Guatemala and Sri Lanka. Some lessons learned during the piloting process in these countries are included in the guide, together with lessons drawn from other types of evaluation. Examples illustrating how the methodology can be applied are also closely based on the methods and results from the pilot work.

PART ONE

THE APPROACH

This guide presents an evaluation framework that assesses the contribution to recovery associated with post-disaster interventions. It is a method focused on assessing positive and negative changes to the lives of affected people and other local stakeholders, in the medium term following a disaster event. The output of the approach is a report that presents detailed findings, an in-depth analysis drawing on the findings, and a concluding section that discusses the contribution to change generated by post-disaster interventions – including a series of summary statements.

The approach assumes that changes in people's well-being and livelihoods can be most clearly identified at a household level. Assessing change necessarily involves identifying what the situation was like for households before and after the disaster occurred, as well as the situation following a period of post-disaster recovery and intervention. We present a technique for collecting retrospective data to cover these changes, combining quantitative and qualitative data collection and analysis.

The approach requires similar levels of staffing and resources as many other types of evaluation. However, although the methodology is structured, it requires key skills in design, field data collection, and interpretative analysis that may not always be available in agency field teams. It may often be advisable to commission a specialist third party to undertake the evaluation: this approach is well suited to a group of agencies acting together to commission the work. Note that the Contribution to Change methodology is designed to complement other evaluation tools; it is not a substitute for process evaluations or audits aimed at examining whether specific project inputs and outputs have been met.

http://dx.doi.org/10.3362/9781780448114.001

Emphasis on evaluating 'contribution'

This guide uses the concept of Contribution to Change to describe the relative importance of post-disaster interventions in aiding people's recovery. This is distinct from a focus on 'attribution', which seeks to establish what specific changes have resulted from an agency's intervention.

This is because the activities of an individual agency, and the effects of those activities, will not normally occur in isolation but rather as part of a multi-layered, complex response by both local and external actors (see 'Example from the field 1'). Social, economic, and political contexts, including the effects of international markets, access to communications, past or present conflicts, and environmental factors, also have a bearing on the final outcomes for a given population following an emergency. Thus it is more realistic in such settings to consider 'contribution' to outcomes or, as some authors prefer, 'contributory impact'.

Example from the field 1: Contribution as more realistic than attribution

In Aceh, Indonesia, after the Indian Ocean tsunami in 2004, some 2,135 schools were destroyed or severely damaged and over 2,500 teachers and education personnel were killed. Such massive disruption to the education system risked undermining the educational prospects of an entire generation of children in Aceh. To prevent this, the Indonesian Ministry of Education and Culture, UNICEF and several non-governmental organizations including CARE International and Save the Children worked together to rebuild schools, train new teachers, and provide educational materials and school feeding programmes. The success of those various initiatives also rested on the efforts and support of teaching staff, parents, and pupils during the recovery period following the disaster. In such situations it would be impossible for a single agency to demonstrate that a given recovery outcome, such as restoration of previous levels of educational attainment, could be directly attributed to its programmes. The best that can be claimed is that they have made a contribution to the overall impact achieved by various initiatives in the sector and by the efforts of the affected population.

The Contribution to Change approach views recovery as depicted in Figure 1. The idea is to try to understand the relative importance of the intervention activities depicted by the bottom arrow (normally this refers to the range of interventions in a given site, though in some instances the method may be applied to a single intervention).

Another important aspect of this approach is the recognition that it is not sufficient to look only at outcomes that have been achieved. An intervention may have contributed in a major way to the change that has occurred, but if that level

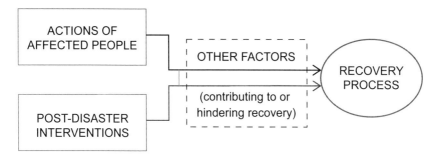

Figure 1   Contribution to Change: what is the relative importance of interventions in recovery?

of change has itself been only limited, there is a danger that the value of the contribution will be exaggerated.

We therefore also need to look at the overall progress of recovery in order to calibrate the contribution that interventions have made to the extent of recovery that has actually been achieved. Both are important aspects of assessing contribution to change.

Concentrating on just the 'intervention' part of the previous diagram, we can depict this distinction as shown in Figure 2.

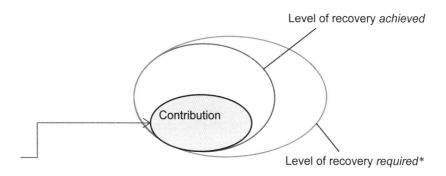

Figure 2   Contribution to Change: achievements versus progress

* We recognize that planned or desirable outcomes may not simply be recovery of former states; however, we need some kind of benchmark level as a gauge – and we can perhaps have a working assumption that at least recovery to the former situation is a desirable outcome.

Assessing contribution is not an easy task. Although we present a systematic methodology for undertaking this type of evaluation, the end results of the analysis require careful interpretation of the evidence collected. We need to look at the effects of the intervention, consider other responses and contributions, and be aware of the effect of external factors and issues in shaping recovery. All these elements need to be included in the analysis and its conclusions presented in the report.

The most important output of the Contribution to Change methodology is a detailed discussion of how these elements have shaped key aspects of people's lives. This will be reflected in what we call the narrative analysis (see Part Three, Step 9) and the conclusions (Step 10), which are set out in the final report (Step 11).

However, one way to provide a shorthand interpretation of contribution is to create Contribution to Change statements (the tool for which is provided in Step 10). This tool generates simple statements about **level of recovery** (the overall progress of recovery) and **contribution to recovery achieved** (the changes that can be linked to interventions), and compares these to create a **Contribution to Change statement** (the contribution of the intervention towards meeting the recovery that is required).

Further reading

On evaluation and contribution

Bamberger, M., Rugh, J. and Mabry, L. (2012) *RealWorld Evaluation: Working under Budget, Time, Data, and Political Constraints*, 2nd edn, Thousand Oaks, CA: Sage Publications.

O'Flynn, M. (2010) *Impact Assessment: Understanding and Assessing our Contributions to Change*, M&E Paper 7, Oxford: INTRAC. <www.intrac.org/data/files/resources/695/Impact-Assessment-Understanding-and-Assessing-our-Contributions-to-Change.pdf> [accessed 17 July 2013].

Proudlock, K., Ramalingam, B. and Sandison, P. (2009) 'Improving humanitarian impact assessment: bridging theory and practice', in ALNAP, *8th Review of Humanitarian Action: Performance, Impact and Innovation*, London: ALNAP. <www.alnap.org/pool/files/8rhach2.pdf> [accessed 17 July 2013].

See also Annex 2.

Other defining elements of the methodology

Focus on livelihood changes at household level

The methodology is rooted in the idea of undertaking analysis at the grass-roots scale in order to reveal the most significant changes in people's lives associated with a disaster and the subsequent 'recovery' period. Recent reviews of evaluation in post-disaster settings argue that it is imperative to ensure that assessing the effects of interventions on the 'lives of affected populations' is at the heart of evaluation (Proudlock et al., 2009).

The intention of the approach is to take a holistic or multi-dimensional view of people's lives – one that looks broadly at different aspects of people's well-being. It is felt that a more holistic evaluation of the changes in people's lives is needed as all too often agency evaluations focus on the components of their own intervention, for example the provision of health services or clean drinking water. The data therefore give a partial picture of the changes in people's lives and may miss crucial information needed in order to assess how well communities have recovered.

It is important not to view disaster impact and recovery narrowly in terms of only income-generating activities. The 'livelihoods' concept is one useful way of thinking about this (see Scoones, 1998). It refers to the range of material and non-material assets and resources to which people have (or do not have) access in order to achieve well-being. This enables recognition of the role that different types of assets have in supporting recovery from disaster situations.

We can consider this level of approach as both normative (in terms of a focus on people's needs/recovery) and instrumental (in terms of agencies' operational objectives – by putting interventions into their social context).

Another important consideration in developing this approach concerns the level at which change is expected to be observed. We have decided to focus on households as the most important location at which changes can be observed. Most core humanitarian and post-disaster recovery interventions – education, health, WASH, shelter, food distribution, nutrition programmes, seed distribution, income generation, cash-based programming, infrastructure redevelopment, etc. – ultimately have impacts that are most likely to be recognized by affected populations if they result in changes in the daily activities and livelihoods of households.

Although the focus is on a household level of analysis, it is usually also important in the evaluation to build in attention to other key social dimensions such as differences in disaster impact and recovery associated with gender, age, ethnicity, caste, and income group. This may require targeting within the data collection design. For example, short- and long-term impacts can play out differently for female-headed households, as well as for women and men at an intra-household level (see Box 3 for a summary of how gender dimensions are approached in this guide).

Box 3 Addressing gender dimensions

There are two basic approaches to considering gender in the context of evaluations of disaster and post-disaster interventions. The first of these can be described as a gender-sensitive approach to evaluation, in which gender dimensions are integrated into data collection and analysis, including the identification and collection of appropriate sex and age disaggregated data (SADD). This is the approach adopted in this guide.

The second approach is a gender-focused approach in which the key focus of evaluation is any change to gender relations and gender equity as a consequence of the disaster and/or post-disaster interventions. Gender-focused approaches require a reorientation of sampling and survey methods, and the use of specific qualitative tools, and are not covered in this guide. However, the tools described in the guide can potentially be modified for this purpose, including sample designs that do not use 'household' as the basic sampling unit.

The timeframe of the approach

The measurement of change necessarily means that data or information about a given change (e.g. to a household's or community's livelihoods) needs to correspond to at least two points of time. In the case of post-disaster interventions, it makes sense to look at three or four points in time, because we need to understand both how the disaster impacted people's livelihoods and how the recovery progressed.

To describe the different points of time that are of interest, we have used the following terminology, which is represented graphically in Figure 3:

* T_{-1} – before the disaster (before the onset of a hazard);

* T_0 – the disaster event (the onset of a hazard – see also Box 4);

* T_{+1} – early post-disaster (after an initial emergency period);

* T_{+2} – late post-disaster (after a recovery phase period).

Because of the interest in livelihood trajectories and because the impacts of a disaster on these may not be immediately assessable, T_{+1} is an important time point in the analysis. Conceptually at least, this is the point when livelihood impacts are considered to be at their greatest, but also the point when recovery actions are seen to commence, including the implementation of post-relief interventions. We recognize that this is a simplification of what happens in reality on the ground, but it serves as a basic conceptual framing for the methodology.

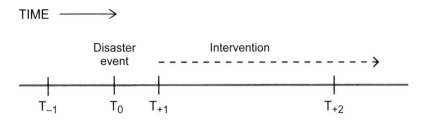

Figure 3   Conceptual timeframe for a rapid-onset disaster

Note: For disasters associated with rapid-onset hazards, the timing of T_0 is more or less fixed. The method can also be applied to slow-onset disasters, but in this case a decision has to be made on the timing of T_0. In many cases this can best be defined as the 'trigger of intervention' – for example the point at which a disaster emergency is formally declared and/or a request for external assistance is made. In a slow-onset disaster, it will also be more complicated and less feasible to assess a 'pre-disaster state', and so the analysis may have to commence at T_0.

The precise timing of T_{-1}, T_{+1} and T_{+2} will depend on the unique context and considerations for evaluation design, but Part Two, Step 2, provides some guideline pointers to help with these decisions. The data collection tools described in Part Two relate in different ways to these four points in time, focusing most on the differences between T_{-1} and T_{+1} (what were the impacts?); T_{+1} and T_{+2} (what have been the responses?); and T_{-1} and T_{+2} (has there been an effective recovery?).

Box 4 Complex timelines

Although the methodology refers to a disaster event (T_0), it is important to recognize that any analysis of actual hazards or disasters is inherently complex, because these 'events' can seldom be reduced to single points in time. Disasters have both ante-cedent conditions and long-term implications, and the responses to them range over time from immediate relief efforts to long-term recovery. Hence, when analysing, it is more accurate to conceive of them as 'processes'.

Also, the picture is complicated by multiple and repeated hazard events. This was borne out during pilot studies where communities often referred to several different events affecting their localities. The 'disaster' that grabs the headlines is not neces-sarily seen as the most significant event by local populations.

However, with careful analysis, the flexibility and mixed-method style of the approach used in this guide should enable both these sets of complexities to be taken into account in evaluation.

Retrospective data collection

The method presented in this guide assumes that primary data collection for the analysis will actually take place at T_{+2}. As discussed in the Introduction, it is seldom the case that detailed baseline data can be collected prior to this point that relates to all aspects of livelihoods and to a basket of interventions.

Given the inherently unpredictable nature of rapid-onset disasters, the chaos that usually ensues, and the need, for humanitarian reasons, to respond urgently, evaluators rarely have the opportunity to identify a clear baseline at the time of the disaster. That means that while data corresponding to T_{+2} can be collected in real time, in most cases data corresponding to T_{-1} or T_{+1} will have to be collected retrospectively, based on the participants' recollection and backed up by any written records that may be available.

Piloting of the surveys has shown that retrospective data can be collected from households, with reasonable confidence in the reliability of those data. Triangulation between sources should reveal discrepancies and unreliable sources can be discarded from the analysis. Nevertheless, to minimize bias, the retrospective data collection ideally should take place within 6 to 12 months, although a balance has to be struck between issues of data recall (see Box 5) and the need to allow enough time for livelihood changes to become manifest.

Box 5 Reliability of memory recall

Research methods such as surveys, interviews, and focus groups usually rely on the assumption that an individual's memory of events or circumstances is generally accurate, coherent, consistent, and reliable. However, psychological research into memory processes indicates that this may not be the case. Memory is a reconstruction of events based on several elements and subject to distortion as well as failure (i.e. forgetting). Research also suggests that recollections tend to be 'broadly true' rather than strictly accurate, and that errors in remembering (such as errors in dates, specific details, and estimations of the duration of events) tend to increase as the time since the event lengthens (Herlihy et al., 2012). In particular, it has been shown that stress, trauma, and depression – all frequently occurring in post-disaster contexts – can influence memory and recall.

As the Contribution to Change methodology depends on surveying and interviewing households to establish retrospective data, it is important to acknowledge that an individual's memory of their situation may not be 100% accurate. Specific details, such as the name of an NGO that provided assistance, or the dates on which that assistance was provided and its duration, need to be verified from more than one source (triangulation). Furthermore, an expectation of 'broadly true' and inconsistencies in individual accounts may be more appropriate than expecting memories to be completely accurate.

In some cases, it may be possible to follow a two-phase data-collection approach, where initial and follow-up data can be collected separately. This will be used when a first visit to the site(s) affected by the disaster can be done one to two months after the event (for the collection of data covering the period T_{-1} to T_{+1}). A follow-up visit can then be done 12 to 15 months after the disaster (for the collection of data covering the period T_{+1} to T_{+2}). Both visits will collect similar data, although questions will need to be modified to reflect the different timings of data collection.

Mixed methods for data collection

The methods and tools described in Part Two and Part Three aim to provide a relatively simple and effective way of identifying the changes at the household level for agencies interested in identifying and documenting credible evidence of their contributions to change.

Any evaluation requires important consideration of the most appropriate methods of gathering data or evidence about livelihoods at the household and community levels. Methods used need to be robust enough to collect credible evidence but simple enough for field application in a range of contexts (see Box 6). The approach proposed in this guide is designed around the use of qualitative and quantitative methods that should be quite familiar to most researchers and evaluators.

Quantitative methods use larger samples and are good for determining the direction and amount of change across a population. Typically, the quantitative methods likely to be useful include:

- household questionnaire surveys;
- community-level questionnaires.

Qualitative approaches usually involve in-depth work with smaller numbers of people. They can bring depth of understanding to the context and processes of change, and can be useful for understanding perspectives on the reasons why a change has or has not occurred. They are also more participatory in terms of providing more opportunities for the 'voice' of disaster-affected populations to be expressed. Typically, the qualitative methods likely to be useful include:

- semi-structured interviews (key informant, household and group interviews);
- participatory techniques (group exercises such as participatory mapping and event timelines).

Recognizing the different advantages and limitations of both qualitative and quantitative research tools, the approach taken in this guide is to recommend the joint use of both qualitative and quantitative methods to develop a more detailed narrative of change.

Where possible, the evaluation should utilize other sources of data such as government records and statistics, agencies' own monitoring and evaluation reporting, and spatial imaging. These may explain, supplement, or provide valuable checks for household-level data (see Part Two, Step 1).

Where possible, during the process of analysis, different sources of data should be compared using the principle of triangulation to verify findings, reveal inconsistencies, and allow consideration of possible sources of bias or inaccuracy. This means that some limited repetition of question themes within different data collection tools and sources is useful.

Box 6 Practicality and flexibility

The approach developed in this guide is a compromise. The evaluation method is robust enough to provide reliable evidence on which to assess contribution to change. However, it does not match the highly rigorous study design accomplished in some evaluation approaches that use very large data sets and complex tools of data collection and analysis. The emphasis is on developing a practical approach that can be implemented relatively cheaply without very high levels of expertise.

This guide does not provide blueprint data collection tools. The approach emphasizes flexibility in the application of tools and the design of questions to fit context and purpose. What is required is that decisions on methodology must be made with a clear logic and rationale.

Further reading

On recall

Herlihy, J., Jobson, L. and Turner, S. (2012) 'Just tell us what happened to you: autobiographical memory and seeking asylum', *Applied Cognitive Psychology* 26: 661–76. <http://dx.doi.org/10.1002/acp.2852>.

On mixed methods

Bamberger, M., Rao, V. and Woolcock, M. (2010) *Using Mixed Methods in Monitoring and Evaluation: Experiences from International Development*, Policy Research Working Paper 5245, Washington, DC: World Bank.

Mertens, D.M. and Wilson, A.T. (2012) *Program Evaluation Theory and Practice: A Comprehensive Guide*, New York, NY: Guilford Press.

Scoones, I. (1998) *Sustainable Rural Livelihoods: A Framework for Analysis*, IDS Working Paper 72, Brighton: Institute of Development Studies.

On integrating gender considerations

Mazurana, D., Benelli, P., Gupta, H. and Walker, P. (2011) *Sex and Age Matter: Improving Humanitarian Response in Emergencies*, Somerville, MA: Feinstein International Center, Tufts University. <http://sites.tufts.edu/feinstein/2011/sex-and-age-matter> [accessed 17 July 2013].

Planning and management

As noted in the Introduction, the Contribution to Change methodology is particularly suited to a multi-agency approach, although it can also be conducted for single agencies. In either case, the management team that is commissioning the work has to make decisions on the scope and scale of the evaluation, and on the roles, responsibilities, and composition of the evaluation team. It is also important to consider at this stage how the outputs of the evaluation are expected to link with other evaluation processes.

Planning and resources

The first considerations relate to the scope and scale of the evaluation. The characteristics of the disaster and of subsequent interventions will largely determine how large-scale and complex the evaluation might be, but the final decision is likely to rest also on cost and staffing requirements. It is critical to understand fully the methodology presented in Part Two and Part Three before coming to these decisions, but, in terms of resource implications, the key factors are the time, staffing, and logistics required for:

- **preliminary work** – initial investigations, data collection design and field preparation (see Part Two, Steps 1–5); in most cases, this will require a small team of senior-level personnel (approximately two to five people, depending on the number of field sites) over a period of four to six weeks;

- **fieldwork** – the main data collection phase using both quantitative and qualitative tools (see Part Two, Step 6); this requires a mixed team of senior- and junior-level personnel (approximately 8 to 20 people, depending on the sample size) over a period of two to six weeks;

- **analysis and write-up** – compiling and analysing the results, developing conclusions, and producing a final report (see Part Three, Steps 7–11). This will require mainly senior staff (approximately two to five people) over a period of four to six weeks.

The calculations of time and cost for the fieldwork phase are likely to be the main concern. To avoid compromising on data quality, we recommend that one person could be expected to work with four households per day on the questionnaire survey, or up to three households per day if undertaking semi-structured interviews (allowing time for travel between selected households, questionnaire checks, and writing up interviews). The full duration of fieldwork then depends on the size of the field team in relation to the size of the sample.

The team

An important question to be resolved at an early stage of the design of evaluation is who will carry out the work. It is possible to use agency field staff, as long as they have the necessary methodological and analytical skills (see below). However, to avoid bias in the data collected and in the interpretation of those results, it is important that the evaluation team is seen to be neutral and can take a neutral perspective on the interventions and their outcomes. For this reason it may be appropriate in many cases to commission a third party to undertake the evaluation. This can be particularly cost-effective in contexts where there is multi-agency inter-vention, where a group of agencies can join forces to commission a single analysis of change. Whether it's in-house or third-party, it is vital that the evaluation team work closely with the management team that is commissioning the work to ensure agreement on evaluation design and to build ownership.

The capacity and field experience of the evaluation team that will conduct the data collection and analysis are key to the success of this approach. The methodology requires a team with personnel that include at a minimum the following skills or attributes:

Skills and knowledge

- knowledge of their interview topic and different interview methods (quantita-tive and qualitative);
- good communication and people skills;
- good listening skills for accurately recording information;
- planning and organizational skills;
- data analysis skills;

Personal qualities

- outgoing, confident, and motivated;
- tactful, polite, and friendly;
- able to put people at ease;
- persistent and patient;
- able to follow instructions;
- accurate and honest when recording information;
- able to keep confidentiality.

The Contribution to Change methodology is such that knowledge and experience in mixed-method research is required. It is important wherever possible to recruit a team of field investigators who know well the social and cultural context of the evaluation site, and who are fully conversant in the local language (see 'Example from the field 2'). It is also important as far as possible to ensure that teams have an appropriate balance of men and women when working with households and communities. In many cultures it may be inappropriate for women to be interviewed by men, and in most contexts women may be better able to elicit accurate responses from women.

Example from the field 2: Appropriate levels of skill

In the pilot conducted in Sri Lanka as part of the process of developing this guide, we worked with staff and students of a local university. For data collection, we found that an effective combination for field research was mid-career researchers with considerable past experience for qualitative work and graduate students with required educational background and experience for undertaking the quantitative surveys.

Links with other evaluative processes

A Contribution to Change evaluation has a specific purpose. It does not directly scrutinize the operations of intervention programmes or look at wider issues such as advocacy. In order to evaluate efficiency, effectiveness, value for money, or other aspects such as environmental impact, agencies have to commission a process or formative evaluation. The results of the Contribution to Change approach should be viewed in parallel with these other types of evaluation.

Good programming at an agency level will have included ongoing monitoring of outputs or results and will have included social (or downward) accountability aspects such as feedback from the affected population. All these data will complement, but not replace, the evidence gained from the Contribution to Change methodology. Agencies have often struggled with providing evidence for impacts when conducting evaluations. The methodology presented here has therefore been designed to help address this deficiency.

Further reading

On planning and management of evaluations

Bamberger, M., Rugh, J. and Mabry, L. (2012) 'Organizing and managing evaluations',
   chapter 17 in *RealWorld Evaluation: Working under Budget, Time, Data, and Political
   Constraints*, 2nd edn, Thousand Oaks, CA: Sage Publications.
Cosgrave, J., Ramalingam, B. and Beck, T. (2009) *Real-time Evaluations of Humanitarian
   Action: An ALNAP Guide. Pilot Version*, London: ALNAP. <www.alnap.org/pool/files/
   rteguide.pdf> [accessed 17 July 2013].

PART TWO

DATA COLLECTION TOOLS AND METHODS

The goal of the Contribution to Change approach is to use on-the-ground investigations within communities to understand the characteristics and processes of recovery from rapid-onset disasters and the role of disaster-related interventions in supporting the change achieved.

In order to do this, we need to investigate:

- what happened to people and their livelihoods as a result of the hazard event, and how life changed from what it was like before;

- what people did in response to the losses, and what help they received;

- what people's livelihood situations are like now, and what accounts for the present situation.

Part Two of the guide provides a recommended set of methods for undertaking these field investigations. Commencing with some of the overall principles for the design of the evaluation, it then describes six steps in the data collection methodology, from preliminary investigations and development of the data collection tools, through preparations for working with communities and sampling procedures, to implementation of data collection in the field.

http://dx.doi.org/10.3362/9781780448114.002

Overall design

Building on Part One, it is important to reiterate three underlying principles of the Contribution to Change approach that have important implications for the data collection design:

- a focus on the changes experienced by people in their lives and livelihoods;

- the use of different methods and data sources to understand these changes and how they occurred;

- an expectation that in most cases data will not be collected during the early stages following a disaster.

These lead to the following key design features:

- **Household-level focus:** Most of the data collection will take place with household representatives, although this will be complemented by group meetings, work with community leaders and other local key informants, and data drawn from secondary sources.

- **Mixed methods:** The quantitative instruments used are likely to consist of a structured household questionnaire survey and a structured community questionnaire. The qualitative instruments used are likely to include interviews with key informants, groups, and individual households, as well as participatory techniques with groups.

- **Retrospective data:** It is assumed that in most cases data will have to be collected retrospectively. The data collection will include both information that will enable the reconstruction of how livelihoods changed immediately after the disaster event and information on how the situation has changed since (therefore covering the period T_{-1} to T_{+1} and T_{+1} to T_{+2}; see Figure 3).

Table 2 indicates the design steps required for undertaking data collection. These steps, 1 to 6, are described in detail in the remainder of Part Two.

Table 2   Steps in design, training, and fieldwork

Step 1	Preliminary investigation	See pages 25–28
Step 2	Quantitative methods design	See pages 29–39
Step 3	Qualitative methods design	See pages 40–47
Step 4	Preparing to work with communities	See pages 48–54
Step 5	Sampling	See pages 55–59
Step 6	Field data collection	See pages 60–64

Note that a minimum period of four to six weeks is likely to be needed prior to the main data collection taking place (for preliminary work, design of data collection tools, training, and field testing). Data collection itself is likely to span two to six weeks (see Part One, 'Planning and management').

Table 2 presents a simple data collection process with one main period of fieldwork followed by analysis, and it is assumed that, for time and cost reasons, most evaluations would follow this linear process. However, a valuable modification to the approach would be to have two successive periods of fieldwork, with time for initial analysis of results before embarking on the second (see Box 7).

Box 7 An alternative, staggered approach to data collection

If time and budget allow, the evaluation can be based on two rounds of full data collection, with an intervening step of initial analysis – the first round to establish patterns of change (impact and recovery), and the second to then build on the initial results in order to investigate the reasons for those specific changes. The value of such an approach is that it can strengthen the conclusions that can be made about the contribution to change.

Although both periods of fieldwork would best utilize a mix of methods, the first could rely quite heavily on survey data and the second could place more emphasis on qualitative methods. Nevertheless, the additional time required for going into the field and for initial analysis is likely to lengthen the duration of the evaluation by four to eight weeks and increase staffing costs accordingly.

Both the quantitative and qualitative instruments recommended in this guide need to be **adapted** to suit the local context, the nature of the disaster, and the types of intervention that have been taking place (see Box 8). For this reason, we do not provide blueprint tools such as pre-designed questionnaires or interview schedules (however, we do provide examples of questions as illustrations).

Box 8 Fitting the tools to the context

It is important that the data collection tools should be broad in scope. However, they cannot investigate all aspects of livelihoods in the same depth; some selectivity is required or else the data collection tools will become too time-consuming to administer. There is likely to be focus in the tools on those sectors of disaster impact/intervention that are of particular importance in the local context. This might relate, for example, to certain types of farming support, shelter, WASH interventions, support for women's enterprise, or disaster preparedness.

Once the design and tools are finalized, some **flexibility** should also be built into the field use of some tools so that there is the potential to add themes that emerge during data collection, such as previously unreported issues that undermine recovery. This should be feasible with qualitative tools. However, it may be more difficult with quantitative tools that are based on standardized pre-printed questionnaires.

All the qualitative and quantitative instruments used in this assessment should be **translated** into the local language and then validated by cross-checking with other local language speakers. This is critically important for the quality of the data collected.

STEP 1

Good evaluation design, including sampling strategies and the construction of data collection tools, will benefit from as much preliminary information as possible. Adequate time and resources must be allocated in order to gather secondary information available, consult government and non-government agencies involved in disaster response and disaster prevention, and undertake initial investigations in the local areas where the main evaluation will take place. This should be undertaken over a period of one to two weeks, prior to designing the data collection tools.

Step 1 will provide information on how to:

- **establish contact with relevant organizations;**

- **identify, access, and collate existing data on the local sites, the disaster impacts, and the interventions;**

- **undertake initial meetings with key organizations, local leaders, and residents of the field sites;**

- **produce a preliminary report to guide the evaluation design.**

1.1 Establish contacts

A first task is to establish contact with key stakeholders at different levels, explaining the purpose and scope of the evaluation. This includes government agencies, non-government organizations, and local authorities in the intended field sites. In most cases it will be necessary to follow a protocol in terms of who to contact and from which authorities to gain permission in order to work in the intended field sites. This will vary from country to country. Engagement of local community leaders is not only likely to be a necessary step but should also facilitate the process of working with households.

1.2 Existing data

Contacts with stakeholders should help in the process of identifying and securing access to existing (or secondary) data to both inform the evaluation design and to feed into the analysis. This may include background information such as census data and reports on socio-economic development, as well as documents relating to the disaster impacts and specific intervention activities. It appears that evaluations often do not make full use of pre-existing project monitoring and survey results compiled by intervention agencies, which can be an important source of data (and particularly useful for triangulation purposes; see Part One, 'Other defining elements of the methodology').

1.3 Initial meetings

In many cases, however, existing reports and data sets will not provide all the insights required for designing the data collection tools, and a series of preliminary meetings are required to fill in the gaps. It is important to undertake initial field visits to the evaluation sites to meet with local leaders and have an initial opportunity to talk with residents. During these brief visits (one day per site should suffice), the idea is to gain a preliminary overview of the socio-economic and ethnic characteristics of the community, recent changes, and challenges (see Box 9), as well as an overview of the disaster and post-disaster situation in question.

Box 9 Cumulative disasters

In hazard-prone situations, it is commonly the case that the impacts of different disasters overlap in time and place, making it difficult to consider single 'events' in isolation. In areas where multiple disasters have occurred sequentially or concurrently, a greater attention may be necessary to the cumulative impact of disasters and the role of interventions in dealing with these as well as the specific effects of the disaster in question.

These multiple events may also include emergencies or livelihood 'shocks' that are not related to rapid-onset hazards, including the effects of conflict or economic crises.

The importance of these additional events should be established as much as possible during the preliminary meetings so that they can be reflected in the tools and carefully considered in the analysis. In the semi-structured interviews, for example, questions can be asked about previous shocks and the extent of recovery from those prior to the disaster, or about the extent to which ongoing crises or new shocks have affected post-disaster recovery.

During these initial visits (just as in subsequent visits), in order to avoid bias in the subsequent data collection it is vital that the investigating team remains as neutral as possible on the subject of interventions, and does not inform or sensitize community members about the activities of agencies.

Effort should also be made to speak to all the organizations that have undertaken post-disaster interventions in the area, to gain information on project activities and, where possible, full lists of beneficiaries (see 'Example from the field 3'). Useful background information on the evaluation sites and the socio-economic context is also likely to arise from meetings with local, district, and national authorities.

1.4 Preliminary report

The findings of these initial discussions and of the review of existing data and documentation should be compiled in a short preliminary report. This should provide a base of information on which to design the data collection phase, including key topics to be included in the questionnaires (Step 2) and semi-structured interviews (Step 3), and information from which to devise the sampling strategy (Step 5). The report should also aim to identify any issues over which there may be high sensitivity in the communities and any sources of risk to the safety of investigators while working in the field (Step 4).

Aspects to include in the report are:

* maps of the sites;

* socio-economic attributes and other characteristics of the communities to be studied, with census statistics if available;

* details of general changes that have taken place in the communities over the last 10 to 15 years, including other disaster events;

* the main impacts of the disaster in question, with statistics if available;

* key aspects of people's livelihoods that are likely to have changed since the disaster;

* the range of post-disaster interventions that have taken place, including details of aid provided and lists of beneficiary households, if available;

* an assessment of key sensitivities, risks to evaluation participants, and risks to field investigators.

If specific case study sites for the evaluation have not yet been identified, the preliminary investigation may also be used as a means to compile information on a range of communities to inform site selection.

Example from the field 3: Distinguishing multiple interventions

In the pilot conducted in Sri Lanka, we found that it was difficult for household respondents to distinguish between the intervention activities of different organizations. Separating out specific interventions is often difficult for people when there are multiple organizations active in the area. This underlines the importance of undertaking prior scoping work to inform field investigators so that they can recognize and confirm with people which intervention they are discussing.

QUANTITATIVE METHODS DESIGN
HOUSEHOLD AND COMMUNITY SURVEYS

Quantitative data can be gathered using different types of surveys. In this guide we focus on the use of household and community surveys. The surveys are undertaken using standardized, pre-designed questionnaires. Each questionnaire is divided into separate modules that gather information on specific topics.

Careful design of a questionnaire is crucial. Adequate time must be given to developing and structuring the questions so that the tool is effective as a way of gaining information, and at the same time is clear and practical to use in the field.

Note that, as for all the data collection tools recommended in this guide, a blueprint for questionnaire design is not provided. Surveys have to be tailor-made for the specific context and case. However, a series of examples of questions that might be used in this approach are provided at the end of this section. These should be considered as illustrative only – questionnaires must be designed to match the context of each evaluation. For more detailed guidelines and tips on question phrasing and questionnaire design in general, see the further reading sources recommended at the end of this step.

Step 2 gives advice on how to:

- **define the main topics to be included in each survey and the overall question-naire design;**

- **work on the specific design of each module, question by question;**

- **integrate the different modules into a complete draft questionnaire;**

- **translate the draft questionnaires (if needed);**

- **pre-test the questionnaire before finalization.**

2.1 Survey topics and design

The decision about the topics to be included in the surveys should involve the full evaluation team and should be made at the same time as question themes are decided for the qualitative work.

In order to ensure that the questionnaire development corresponds to the evaluation objective, create a matrix that lists:

•   what information is needed for the evaluation;

•   why the organization needs to know this;

•   who can tell evaluators this information;

•   how to find the information.

This will help in assessing what is needed from each type of survey (see Box 10) and what topics are more appropriate for qualitative methods (see Step 3). The preliminary investigations (Step 1) should provide important information to help answer these questions.

Potential topics might include categories such as income, housing/shelter, education, health, labour, migration, social networks, government programmes, and disaster risk management. They should then be ranked in order of importance. Topics with low priority should be dropped if there are difficulties in including them all. This is likely to be the case if there is a need to keep a questionnaire down to a reasonable length.

The selected topics will form modules in the questionnaire.

When deciding the overall design, the team should take into account not only the aims of the survey, but also practical issues such as the capacity for collecting data, the funding available, and the amount and quality of data available from other sources.

In order not to over-burden survey respondents (and jeopardize the quality of the data collected), questionnaires should be expected to take 45–60 minutes. Piloting found that a household questionnaire with 12–15 modules and a total of 120–150 question responses should take no longer than 60 minutes.

Box 10 The questionnaire types

Community survey

The community survey is designed to collect general information about the community for a better understanding of the local context. The purpose of conducting a community survey is to get an overview of the characteristics of the sites and how and why they have changed over time. The questionnaire used is likely to obtain basic information on at least the following:

- physical communal assets (e.g. infrastructure, health clinics, schools, transport);
- social trends (e.g. patterns of migration);
- economic sectors and employment;
- basic commodity prices;
- government programmes and non-governmental programmes present at the site (including post-disaster interventions).

Household survey

The overall aim of the household surveys is to understand changes in the socio-economic characteristics of the residents of the affected area – especially how lives and livelihoods have changed since the disaster and the factors that seem to be associated with these changes, including the role of interventions. The survey should be designed with the goal of attempting to show changes in economic, health, social, and other relevant status at the household level.

The household survey questionnaire is likely to cover some or all of the topics listed below:

- household 'roster' (names, sex, relationships, ages);
- education (schooling, attendance);
- health (illness, nutrition/food security);
- physical assets (housing, water/sanitation facilities, access to land, animals, items such as boats, nets, ploughs, etc.);
- economic livelihood (working/non-working household members, occupations, labour participation);
- financial assets and income (sources of income, income shocks, debt, assets, wages);
- social factors (migration, social networks);
- interventions (assistance received by sector and source, perceptions of benefit).

Some of the questions will refer to the household as a whole, but others require specific data for individual members of each household. Separating out the responses in this way will also allow for disaggregation of parts of the data set according to gender and age.

2.2 Modules and questions

The next step is to develop a draft questionnaire, module by module. First decide whether each module will address one or more aspects of the topic (for instance, in the module on health, whether you will be asking overall questions on health or separate questions about children's, adults', and older people's health). Then decide on a list of variables that will be measured in order to address each topic effectively. These variables will be represented by specific questions in the survey.

Variables might be phrases such as sources of household incomes, number of people working in the household, amount earned, main occupation (for income), roof and wall materials, occupancy status, house size, and access to services (for housing). It is important to confirm that the specific variables are addressing the key objectives of the evaluation. This is an essential exercise as it enables identification of those variables that are not necessary and can therefore be dropped.

A good starting point for these variables could be the indicators that agencies are already using, for example within a project or sector logical framework. But it is important not to be confined to these indicators if they do not provide the broad picture of household well-being expected in this approach.

For each indicator, one or more questions need to be designed and carefully worded. The specific questions will be designed using information collected in the preliminary investigations (Step 1), such as information on what are the most relevant crops and what support has been available in the locality. Of course, in practice, some of this information may also already be held by organizations undertaking post-disaster interventions.

When defining questions, it is useful to think in terms of three different types:

* questions about facts or behaviour: characteristics of people, things they have done, events, actions they have taken;

* questions of knowledge: what people know, e.g. their awareness about an activity or intervention;

* questions about attitudes: people's opinions, e.g. about the progress of recovery or the effectiveness of intervention.

Questions need to be phrased clearly, simply, and unambiguously. There is generic guidance available on how to phrase questions (see 'Further reading' at the end of this section and Annex 2).

It is particularly important for this retrospective methodology that the time period for the question is clearly specified (see Box 11), because the household survey and the community survey should be designed to gather past and present data simultaneously. Some elements of the questionnaires will have three time points, corresponding to T_{-1}, T_{+1} and T_{+2} (see Part One, Figure 3).

Box 11 Retrospective timing considerations

When collecting data from households, it is important to convey clearly to people what stages in time are being asked about (for example, for T_{-1} an interviewer might state this as 'one month before the flood', and for T_{+1} as 'two weeks after' or 'one month after'). These time points do not always have to be defined precisely, and can refer to brief time periods rather than specific dates; respondents just need to have a clear indication of what those time periods are. In some cases it may be possible to use memorable events such as festivals or religious ceremonies to help people orient their recall of past situations (if the dates of those events are a close match to the relevant time periods).

For retrospective analysis, there may be an issue over deciding the timing of T_0, and hence T_{+1}, for prolonged hazard events such as multi-phase floods. One solution can be to consider T_0 as the time when the hazard was at its worst and T_{+1} for the period immediately after that (e.g. within two weeks). The 'worst' period may in some circumstances be clearly identifiable; in others, we have to rely on individuals' own perception of when the hazard was most acute.

2.3 Draft questionnaire

The questionnaire should be neatly and clearly set out on the pages, so that it is easy for the field researcher to read out the questions and enter the responses in the relevant boxes.

It is important at this stage to think about a system for data entry after questionnaires have been completed. The questionnaire front cover information and the structure of the data entry program should reflect a coding and labelling strategy that maintains consistent, unique identifiers for the observations. A simple and efficient way to do the coding is to assign a letter that will identify the section, followed by a number that will identify the question number in that section. For instance, question 13 of section B will be coded B13. This system will make it easier to discuss specific questions among the team (during training, for example) as well as aid data entry and analysis.

The first modules in the questionnaire should consist of questions that are relatively easy to answer and questions about topics that are not sensitive. A common choice is to set the household roster (information on the members of the household – names, ages, relationships, etc.) as the first module, since basic information on household members is usually not a sensitive topic. It is a good idea to place more sensitive question modules towards the end of the questionnaire, giving the field investigator more time to gain the trust and confidence of the respondent.

2.4 Translation

After the first draft of the questionnaire has been prepared, it often needs to be translated into local languages for pre-testing. Translation is a critical stage of the survey cycle and if poorly undertaken may lead to serious problems. Field testing will help identify some of these problems in good time.

Translation is doubly difficult in cases where there is no written form of a language (see 'Example from the field 4'). In these cases it is important that the survey team develops a standardized way of expressing questions, and that this wording is memorized.

Example from the field 4: Non-written languages

During piloting in Guatemala, the field team spent considerable time discussing how to express some of the questions in the local indigenous language, which was not a written language. There was often disagreement among the team about which words to use, as in some cases there was no exact translation and alternative ways of expressing the questions could lead to different interpretations.

2.5 Pre-testing

Pre-testing is an essential step in the finalization and preparation of the survey. Ideally this should be conducted in an area that is outside the evaluation site (or at least not within the intended sampling population; see Step 5), but has similar characteristics of disaster impact and intervention. Pre-testing the questionnaire is crucial in order to assess the appropriateness of the whole questionnaire design and to assess how well the questions are likely to be interpreted by the interviewers.

Further reading

On survey design

Blair, J., Czaja, R.F. and Blair, E.A. (2013) *Designing Surveys: A Guide to Decisions and Procedures*, Thousand Oaks, CA: Sage Publications.

Iarossi, G. (2006) *The Power of Survey Design: A User's Guide for Managing Surveys, Interpreting Results, and Influencing Respondents*, Washington, DC: World Bank.

Examples of survey question construction

Community survey

G. INFRASTRUCTURE (WATER)

1. Which were the three main sources of drinking water for the community one month before the floods? (Rank in order of importance. See codes)

1st	2nd	3rd

2. Which were the three main sources of drinking water for the community two weeks after the floods?

1st	2nd	3rd

3. Which have been the three main sources of drinking water for the community in the last two weeks?

1st	2nd	3rd

Codes for Q1–3
Piped water = 1, Hand pump = 2, Motorized pumping / Tube well = 3,
Open well = 4, Closed well = 5, Pond = 6, Canal/ River/ Stream = 7,
Spring = 8, Other = 77

Household survey

D. LIVESTOCK OWNED BY MEMBERS OF THIS HOUSEHOLD

Animal	1. Did any of the household members own any of the following animals **one month before the floods**?	2. Did any of the household members own any of the following animals **two weeks after the floods**?	3. Do any of the household members own any of the following animals **now**?	4. How many animals did your household own **one month before the floods**?	5. How many animals did your household own **two weeks after the floods**?	6. How many animals does your household own **now**?
	1 = Yes 2 = No > next animal	1 = Yes 2 = No > next animal	1 = Yes 2 = No > next animal	Number	Number	Number
1 – Bull						
2 – Cow						
3 – Buffalo						
4 – Sheep						
5 – Goat						
6 – Pig						
7 – Poultry						
8 – Other						

H. LABOUR PARTICIPATION (FOR RESPONDENT)

1.	2.	3.	4.	5.	6.	7.	8.	9.
Were you working **one month before the floods?**	What was your main occupation?	Was this a:	Were you working **two weeks after the floods?**	What was your main occupation?	Was this a:	Have you been working in the **last two weeks?**	What has been your main occupation?	Has this been a:
	[codes defined according to context]	(select only one)		[codes defined according to context]	(select only one)		[codes defined according to context]	(select only one)
1 = Yes		Full-time job ⌷	1 = Yes		Full-time job ⌷	1 = Yes		Full-time job ⌷
2 = No > **Q4**		Part-time job ⌷	2 = No > **Q7**		Part-time job ⌷	2 = No > **next section**		Part-time job ⌷
		Occasional job ⌷			Occasional job ⌷			Occasional job ⌷
		Seasonal migrant job ⌷			Seasonal migrant job ⌷			Seasonal migrant job ⌷
		Seasonal job ⌷			Seasonal job ⌷			Seasonal job ⌷
		Work abroad ⌷			Work abroad ⌷			Work abroad ⌷

H. LABOUR PARTICIPATION (FOR PARTNER)

1. Were you working **one month before the floods**? 1 = Yes 2 = No > **Q4**	2. What was your main occupation? **[codes defined according to context]**	3. Was this a: (select only one) Full-time job |_| Part-time job |_| Occasional job |_| Seasonal migrant job |_| Seasonal job |_| Work abroad |_|	4. Were you working **two weeks after the floods**? 1 = Yes 2 = No > **Q7**	5. What was your main occupation? **[codes defined according to context]**	6. Was this a: (select only one) Full-time job |_| Part-time job |_| Occasional job |_| Seasonal migrant job |_| Seasonal job |_| Work abroad |_|	7. Have you been working in the **last two weeks**? 1 = Yes 2 = No > **next section**	8. What has been your main occupation? **[codes defined according to context]**	9. Has this been a: (select only one) Full-time job |_| Part-time job |_| Occasional job |_| Seasonal migrant job |_| Seasonal job |_| Work abroad |_|

K. ASSISTANCE RECEIVED

Post-disaster aid programme [codes defined according to context]	1. Has the household received benefits from the following programme **after the floods**? 1 = Yes 2 = No	2. How often did you receive assistance? 1 = Weekly 2 = Monthly 3 = Quarterly 4 = Bi-annually 5 = Annually 6 = One-off payment	3. When did you first receive assistance?		4. When was the last time you received assistance?		5. What would you estimate was the total value of the assistance? **[use local currency]**	6. How important has the aid received through this programme been for achieving the current state of your housing/ livelihood? 1 = Very important 2 = Quite important 3 = Of little importance
			Month	Year	Month	Year		
Prog. I (housing)								
Prog. II (housing)								
Prog. III (agriculture)								
Prog. IV (agriculture)								
Prog. V (labour)								

STEP 3

The objective of the qualitative work is to explore the perception of changes in livelihoods and living conditions following disaster events, how these changes occurred, and why they are important. Qualitative data collection and analysis are particularly suited for answering *how* and *why* questions – and complement the detailed description of changes that can be achieved through the questionnaire surveys.

The following qualitative tools are the main techniques that can be used:

- key informant interviews;
- household interviews;
- group interviews;
- group exercises.

This step describes how to:

- **decide what the question themes should be for qualitative investigation;**
- **select the themes that are most appropriate for different types of interviews;**
- **design question schedules for interviews;**
- **select and design any additional group exercises.**

3.1 Qualitative question themes

The first task is to decide which themes are best suited for qualitative work. Some thematic overlap with the quantitative work is useful for triangulation, but it is likely that different types of information will be sought from the two sets of methods. Qualitative methods provide the opportunity to gain more in-depth information about key topics. They can probe for more explanatory detail about events and changes, especially the reasons for those changes, and can include direct questions about the role and importance of interventions.

Because the aim of qualitative data collection is to prompt people to explain their perspectives and speak at length, the number of question themes that it is feasible to cover is quite limited. Question themes should be chosen that are most relevant to the specific context of the evaluation.

The following themes might commonly be selected for the qualitative work:

General themes

- problems and challenges faced by the community;

- recent changes and events affecting the community's development;

- external interventions (in general);

- experience of natural hazards;

Disaster-impact themes

- the main impacts of the event or hazard (short term);

- the main impacts of the event or hazard (longer term);

- what people did in response to the impacts (emergency phase);

- relief interventions (emergency phase);

Recovery and contribution themes

- people's longer-term responses (recovery phase);

- community-level responses (recovery phase);

- external post-disaster interventions (recovery phase);

- disaster risk-reduction activities;

- perceptions of the progress of recovery;

- perceptions of the relative contribution of interventions;

- the effects of previous or ongoing events or hazards on recovery;

- other factors affecting the progress of recovery.

The following question themes might also be incorporated; however, because they focus on understanding social differences in the post-disaster experience, it is difficult to address these themes adequately without conducting a larger number of interviews (see Step 5):

- differences in recovery experiences within the community (e.g. by occupation or ethnicity);

- differences in recovery experiences within the household (e.g. by gender or age);

- equity in access to interventions (see Box 12).

Box 12 Considerations of equity

Targeted interventions may also have equity dimensions. Issues of equity in the distribution of assistance can most readily be analysed through qualitative work, and if significant equity problems are raised during preliminary investigations there may be a need to build more emphasis on group interviews into the evaluation design to explore this theme. Alternatively, equity and targeting procedures can be more comprehensively assessed via parallel evaluations.

3.2 Matching themes to interview types

Once a list of question themes has been identified, it is important to think through which interview method is best suited to answer them. Box 13 describes three main kinds of interview that can be utilized for this methodology. They are referred to generally as semi-structured interviews because each is based on a set of questions (or interview schedule), but the use of those questions is not rigidly structured as it would be in a questionnaire survey.

There is no need for a complete division of themes between the different interview types. Indeed, it is important to use the different interview types to compare the perspectives that emerge. However, different types of interview can be used to address a slightly different mix of themes or parts of themes, as shown in the examples below:

- Key informant interviews are useful for gaining **general information** about the issues facing communities, impacts of the disaster, assistance provided, types of short- and long-term intervention, and aspects of governance. Key informants generally have a good level of knowledge of general themes and can usually place these within a wider political and social context.

- Household interviews are the best way to find out detail of the **individual experiences** of **livelihood impact and recovery and how they vary** between households. There should be only brief information on household characteristics. Questions should focus on finding out what people regard as the main immediate and longer-term impacts of the event, what they did to protect their households and to recover, and what type of assistance they received. Sub-questions should be asked to encourage people to explain the how and why aspects of these themes.

- Group interviews are good for probing for more detail into the **impacts and response across the community**, including themes such as impacts on infrastructure and the local economy, impacts on services, community coping strategies, patterns of recovery, and disaster risk reduction. By discussing these things as a group, stronger insights often emerge.

Box 13 Types of interview

Key informant interviews

These are interviews with specific people targeted because of their special role or authority in the community or local area, and/or the specialist knowledge they can provide that relates to the community as a whole. Guiding questions can be drawn from a predefined question list for key informant interviews, but selected depending on what is appropriate to the expertise and role of the person.

Such people may include community leaders, local disaster management coordinators, primary health staff, schoolteachers, and members of grass-roots groups such as local producers' cooperatives or community-based development organizations. In some situations, local-level government staff or NGO field officers may also be included as key informants. It is important to remember, however, that key informants are not neutral interviewees: the perspectives they provide should be treated as opinions, just like those of any other interviewee.

Household interviews

These are in-depth interviews with household members, and typically they make up the majority of the semi-structured interviews undertaken during data collection. The idea is that by speaking with individual households, a full range of people's own experiences and perspectives on change can be recorded.

Normally, the interview takes place with one or more adult members of the household, and the sampling design can stipulate that women and men are represented equally (see Step 5). The selection of households should be broadly representative of the diversity within the community, but because of the relatively small number of interviewees, some purposive sampling may be needed to ensure, for example, that the experiences of those most affected by disasters are adequately recorded (see Step 5).

Group interviews

Group interviews entail bringing together small groups of people (ideally 4 to 10 per group) to jointly discuss interview questions. The idea is that the group setting may help bring out discussion on themes that may be difficult for individuals to work through in one-to-one interviews, or provide a chance to discuss themes from a community-wide perspective, such as disaster impacts on infrastructure, or the management of intervention projects.

A series of group interviews should be undertaken per community (e.g. four to six). It is normally important to split groups according to gender, and it may be important to have separate groups according to other social dimensions such as age, occupation, wealth, or ethnicity, depending on the social characteristics of the community. This separation helps to avoid domination of group discussions by the most powerful or vociferous social groups. Where possible, it can also be useful to split groups according to whether or not they have received the various types of aid.

3.3 Question schedules

It is normally good practice to develop standardized question 'schedules' for each interview type. Once field tested and finalized (in conjunction with the field testing of surveys; see Step 2), these should be printed and ideally laminated so that they can be taken into the field and consulted during the interviews.

Aim to cover around 8 to 12 question themes in each interview. Each of the main questions may have several sub-questions, but try in general to keep to between one and four sub-questions. Question schedules that are longer than this are likely to demand too much of an interviewee's time and patience, given that the idea behind semi-structured interviews is also to ask follow-up questions to clarify or expand on the things that people mention. The aim should be to complete most interviews within one hour.

One example of a question schedule is shown at the end of this section; this indicates how question themes can be translated into interview questions. It is important to view these only as example questions – the precise questions and their wording should be adapted for each context, as part of the data collection design for the specific evaluation.

As with surveys, careful attention should be paid to the wording of the questions to make sure that they are relevant, easily understandable, and unambiguous (see also Box 14). Because of the more conversational nature of in-depth interviews, the researchers using question schedules may not always ask them in exactly the same way; however, encouraging them to follow the agreed phrasing of questions as closely as possible will help to standardize the types of response given and make analysis easier.

Note that, although questions will be asked about periods before, during, and after the disaster event, because the qualitative methodology does not set out to undertake quantified comparisons over time there is less focus on specifying T_{-1} and T_{+1} than there is within the questionnaire survey (see Step 2).

Box 14 Encouraging reflective thought

As well as asking people to describe impacts and responses, some questions should be phrased deliberately to encourage people to think through the issue. The following examples are some questions that can be used in group interviews:

- What have you done as a community that has helped you recover since the [disaster event]?
- How important has that been? Why?
- What assistance has been provided from outside in the period since the [disaster event]?
- How has this helped the community?
- Have there been any problems or negative side effects with the assistance?
- Were you consulted about what you needed? By whom?
- What were the most important changes in this recovery period?
- What or who was mainly responsible for bringing about those changes?
- Was there anything that made it difficult for the community to cope and recover?
- Has anything been done to reduce the effects of future hazards?

3.4 Group exercises

Some additional data-gathering tools may be useful when working with groups, making use of the range of techniques developed under Participatory Rural Appraisal (PRA) and related approaches. Techniques such as participatory mapping, event timelines, transect walks, and ranking and sorting exercises may be particularly useful mechanisms for gaining overview information and for building rapport with community members.

The wide range of established techniques are not discussed in detail here, and evaluation teams are recommended to consult the resources on participatory evaluation listed in Annex 2. Some of these techniques are designed for work with particular groups: for example, there are child-focused methods using drawing and drama. Others utilize images or objects for use with non-literate societies.

The utility and appropriateness of these techniques are highly dependent on social and cultural contexts. However, experience from the pilots undertaken in the development of this guide suggests that two exercises in particular can be useful during the initial stages of fieldwork.

Timelines

Asking groups of people to develop event timelines can be a useful way of identifying other major events (positive and negative) that have affected communities, and of understanding how the disaster in question fits into this sequence of events.

One method is to start with a large sheet of paper with an arrow across the centre to represent time up to the present. Participants are then invited to plot the date of major events along this line, using coloured pens. The researchers can ask questions about the significance and implications of these events as the exercise progresses.

Hazard mapping

Working with community members to draw maps of the locality can be another useful way to gain insights into the distribution of hazard impacts and the location and distribution of interventions. It can also reveal the existence of issues affecting selected parts of the site that might otherwise be overlooked.

Although there is usually no problem engaging people in discussions about what took place where, encouraging people to actively draw and annotate maps can be difficult, and often requires some coaxing at first.

One method is to begin by drawing a key landmark (e.g. a church or community hall) near the centre of a large sheet of paper, and adding a few other features such as main roads and watercourses. People should then be encouraged to add further details, including village boundaries, areas of housing, and agricultural land. Next, people should be asked to plot and explain how the hazard event affected the site, showing the extent of damage and/or the worst affected areas. A final set of annotations can be used to plot the locations and distribution of interventions.

Further reading

On qualitative data collection

Bamberger, M., Rugh, J. and Mabry, L. (2012) 'Qualitative evaluation approaches', chapter 13 in *RealWorld Evaluation: Working under Budget, Time, Data, and Political Constraints*, 2nd edn, Thousand Oaks, CA: Sage Publications.

Patton, M.Q. (2002a) *Qualitative Evaluation and Research Methods*, 3rd edn, Thousand Oaks, CA: Sage Publications, pp. 207–339.

Example of a question schedule for interviews

HOUSEHOLD INTERVIEW QUESTIONS

1. In your household:
   a. What are the ages and gender of household members?
   b. What are the main occupations/income sources?

The immediate emergency

2. How were you immediately affected by the floods?
   a. Injury and illness to household members
   b. Loss/damage of house, belongings
   c. Loss of crops/livestock
   d. Evacuation/displacement
   e. Other immediate impacts

3. What did you do to cope with [the impacts noted above] at that time?

4. Who gave you immediate assistance (during the floods) and what assistance did they provide?

Changes in the period since

5. Please explain the most difficult/important problems your household faced in the month after the floods (for income, health, schooling, transport, etc.).

6. Are you still experiencing or feeling the effects of the floods? How?

7. Have you been able to:
   a. Restore your livelihood? How?
   b. Change to a new livelihood? What is that?
   c. Replace or rebuild damages or losses? How?
   d. Recover from any other effects that you mentioned? How?

8. In the period since the floods, who gave you assistance from within the community?
   a. When and what sort of help?
   b. How useful was it?

9. In the period since the floods, who gave you assistance from outside the community (i.e. government, NGOs, other agencies)?

   For each assistance noted above:
   a. When and what sort of help?
   b. How useful was it?
   c. How much of a difference has this outside help made to you? How and why?

STEP 4

Working at ground level with households and local-level stakeholders requires a number of further considerations that should be built into the evaluation design and data collection practice. If fieldwork is to be successful, it needs to take into account the limitations and expectations of the community. Explicit attention should be paid to ethical principles and risk assessment, and careful thought should be given to how to build trust and rapport. This should all be incorporated into the training for field investigators, together with training and practice in undertaking the data collection methods.

Step 4 describes how to:

• develop ethical guidelines for data collection;

• plan the process of fieldwork in conjunction with community leaders;

• consider how to build trust and rapport with community members;

• undertake a risk assessment;

• provide adequate training for field investigators.

4.1 Ethics

An ethical approach should be followed in all interactions with participants. Some organizations will have formal ethical guidelines and approval processes that need to be followed. For other situations, the ethical code may be informal, but no less important. At a minimum, ethical considerations should include the principles of informed consent and sensitivity in questioning people, together with respect for people's rights to anonymity and privacy (see Box 15).

A standardized approach to informed consent is not only important ethically but also serves as an introduction to the subsequent interview and can improve trust. Participants need to understand what they are being asked to do, by whom, and why.

They need to understand that the data will be used to evaluate the contribution that interventions have made to changing people's lives following the disaster. Where appropriate, participants can be given an information sheet and asked to sign a consent form (but both must be translated into the local language). In other cases, including situations where individuals are non-literate, information statements can be read and participants asked to give verbal consent.

Box 15 An ethical approach

General ethical principles for data collection include the following:

Informed consent

All data should be collected on the basis of informed consent. It is essential that the researcher fully explains the purpose, independence, and outputs of the project to the participant before the questionnaire or interview commences – in clear and simple language (avoiding technical terms and jargon). Participants need to confirm that they understand, and give consent to the collection and use of data (including opinions, perspectives, and explanations) that they provide.

Sensitivity

In all interactions, care must be taken to minimize distress. This can be achieved in part through informing people of question themes in advance and seeking their agreement to continue with those themes. Participants should not be pressed to answer any questions that create distress, and should be completely free to end the dialogue whenever they wish.

Anonymity

Unless otherwise agreed, it should be assumed that people do not wish to be named in evaluation reports and that the statements and perspectives they provide should be anonymized. That means that somebody reading the report should not be able to identify who said what.

Privacy

As a general rule, when conducting interviews it is important that the respondent is able to speak in private – both to protect their views from being overheard by others and to encourage people to speak more freely about their personal information and concerns. As far as possible, the fieldwork should be planned so that interviews can take place in private places. In practice, however, privacy can be difficult to arrange, often because such places are not available. In such cases, the researcher should try to find a compromise; explain to the interviewee that it is best to use a location where disturbance from others can at least be minimized.

Sensitivity to the shocks and experiences people have undergone is a critical ethical principle in an evaluation of this type. Working with those affected by disaster inevitably carries the risk of causing emotional distress. It is important to note that sensitivities may also exist around experiences of external intervention. Try to understand as much as possible about the history of crises and intervention in the area from the preliminary investigations (Step 1), and then discuss these issues among the full field team. A clear protocol for minimizing and dealing with distress should be understood by all before fieldwork commences. At a minimum, training should include recognizing signs of distress and trauma, guidance on how to respond in such situations (including modifying, pausing, or ceasing data collection), strategies for ensuring that interviews conclude positively and do not overemphasize negative outcomes, and guidance on the circumstances in which to refer participants for assistance or support (and on the services available).

In most circumstances, the Contribution to Change approach involves working with adults. However, if the evaluation will also include interviews with children, certain considerations need to be taken into account. The interviewer should be already trained or experienced in interviewing children and, for some agencies, may require clearance to do so. Permission should be sought from parents before interviews take place and parents should also have a right to veto certain questions if they feel that they are inappropriate (see 'Further reading' at the end of this section for more information).

4.2 Community engagement in planning

Planning for data collection should include consultation with local community leaders. In many cases prior permission will be required from them to undertake the surveys and interviews, but consultation can also be important as a step in facilitating the process of data collection and, ultimately, in improving the quality of the data collected. Ideally, through meeting with a group of such people, it will be possible to identify key individuals to work with, who are both ready and willing to assist and are held in a position of trust by other community members.

Such people can advise on key aspects of logistics, such as when to visit households and whether there may be accommodation available for fieldwork teams. It is important to identify the best times of the day to work, in order to ensure that people will be available at home and that excessive demands are not placed on their normal working times. For group interviews, there may be certain days in the week when people are most free to give up their time.

One common habit of evaluation teams is to travel daily into communities during the fieldwork period, while based at accommodation elsewhere. There may be many good reasons why this is so, but it is also useful to consider staying overnight in sites, especially in rural villages. This is likely to keep costs down, as well as improve the quality of the relationship with villagers.

4.3 Building trust and rapport

Collecting good-quality data is inevitably difficult if attention has not been paid to gaining the trust and goodwill of people in the communities. It is generally the case that people welcome the opportunity to express themselves – to have a voice. However, this willingness cannot be taken for granted.

Guidelines for working with communities in order to build rapport with local people typically include:

- making sure that appropriate contacts are made with local leaders;
- being honest and open about the purposes of the work;
- respecting customs about dress and behaviour;
- being flexible about timings and arrangements of meetings with people;
- behaving at all times in a friendly and respectful manner.

Gender and ethnicity considerations are important in this respect. In many situations it is preferable that female investigators undertake work with women. It is also preferable if at least some members of the evaluation team come from the same ethnic group or geographical area of the community. An example of building rapport is given in 'Example from the field 5'.

A problem can arise if people in the community presume that participation in the evaluation will bring direct benefit. This can create tensions, especially among those who are not invited to take part. It can be especially difficult when working with small populations where a high proportion of people are to be included in the sample. In such cases it is especially important to emphasize the purpose and independence of the evaluation to key informants and other respondents, and to take time to explain the sampling procedure (see Step 5).

Example from the field 5: Building trust and rapport

In a pilot study in Sri Lanka, the presence of one member in the team with prior contacts with local officials and community leaders established through the preliminary study facilitated the team's entry to the villages.

Employing field researchers from the local university who could speak Tamil in the local dialect facilitated rapport building, and helped avoid creating unnecessary expectations on the part of the respondents.

The community mapping exercise was a useful participatory tool for securing community inputs towards the identification of sites of flood impact and for initiating the subsequent data collection procedures in the selected villages.

Gender balance in the team was another positive feature that facilitated rapport building with male and female respondents.

The field investigators found that people generally started answering questions with enthusiasm, but there was a danger that this would wane during the questionnaire. One way round that problem was to encourage people to continue working at the same time as being asked questions.

4.4 Risk assessment

Before undertaking fieldwork in the communities it is important also to undertake a risk assessment to ensure the safety of the field investigators. Information on which to base the risk assessment can come from the preliminary investigations (Step 1).

Prior to going into the field, at a minimum all field staff should be made aware of:

- organizational roles, contacts, and communication plans associated with field safety and security;

- specific or general threats or hazards associated with particular fieldwork sites;

- procedures to minimize the most significant risks, for example:

    - malaria prevention;

    - vehicle travel guidelines;

    - guidelines for working in communities such as working in pairs, ensuring adequate communication, and returning from the field before dark;

- guidelines on how to respond to an emergency, including emergency contact information for a hospital and the police;

- field safety equipment, including a first aid kit.

A useful source of practical guidance on safety and security in the field is Bickley (2010).

4.5 Training and practice

Effective training for those undertaking the data collection is essential. A minimum of two days should be allocated for training and practice of the field team, but preferably up to four days should be available to cover all aspects of data collection and preparation, including the preparation of field notes for qualitative work (see Step 6).

Training should commence with an overview of the purpose, scope, and approach of the evaluation. It should include sessions on ethical guidelines (e.g. including the use of informed consent materials), guidelines on working effectively with communities to build rapport, and management of fieldwork risks (see 4.4 'Risk assessment').

Intensive training should then take place for the survey team and for the team carrying out the qualitative work (assuming that separate personnel are assigned to the surveys and the semi-structured interviews; see Part One, 'Planning and management').

It is important that the **quantitative** field staff are trained on the objectives of the surveys. They need to know the purpose of collecting the information, and how it will be used in the evaluation. A critical and engaged field team can contribute substantially to ensuring that the survey tools are compatible for fieldwork. The trainer should then guide the team through the questionnaires, section by section, explaining how to conduct the questioning and how to fill in the survey form.

The **qualitative** team should similarly be introduced to the rationale behind the three different forms of interview, and their corresponding question themes. The trainer should then explain in detail the semi-structured interview process, including listening and responding to answers, asking follow-up questions, using prompts to aid interviewees during discussion, ensuring that question responses relate to the whole household, and note-taking or recording (see Step 6).

The training should have a large practice component. Interviews should be conducted within the classroom as well as with actual households in a 'real' context. For example, the teams could take turns in asking questions to each other in a classroom setting; this can include recording and playing back the practice interviews, with all trainees commenting on what they thought had gone well or not. This should be followed by a field trip, where a few households could be interviewed by the trainees (see Box 16).

The training and field practice should also be seen as another opportunity to refine the questionnaire and question schedules. Finalization and printing of survey forms should take place after this.

Box 16 Field practice

Field practice is the practical part of the training for both quantitative and qualitative data collection. After having classroom-based theoretical training, the field investigators should be taken to a community that has agreed to host practice interviews using the questionnaires or question schedules. The respondents for the field practice should be similar to those targeted in the actual data collection, although preferably the practice should not be conducted in one of the evaluation sites. The trainers should be present at all times to guide and assist the trainees.

Further reading

On ethical approaches and working with vulnerable populations

Bamberger, M., Rugh, J. and Mabry, L. (2012) 'Ensuring competent and ethical practice in the conduct of the evaluation', chapter 9 in *RealWorld Evaluation: Working under Budget, Time, Data, and Political Constraints*, 2nd edn, Thousand Oaks, CA: Sage Publications.

Ellsberg, M. and Heise, L. (2005) *Researching Violence against Women: A Practical Guide for Researchers and Activists*, Washington, DC: World Health Organization, Program for Appropriate Technology in Health (PATH). <www.path.org/publications/files/GBV_rvaw_complete.pdf> [accessed 17 July 2013].

On interviewing children

UNICEF (2002) *Children Participating in Research, Monitoring and Evaluation (M&E) – Ethics and Your Responsibilities as a Manager*, Evaluation Technical Notes No. 1, New York, NY: UNICEF. <www.unicef.org/evaluation/files/TechNote1_Ethics.pdf> [accessed 17 July 2013].

On safety and security in the field

Bickley, S. (2010) *Safety First: A Safety and Security Handbook for Aid Workers*, London: Save the Children UK. <www.eisf.eu/resources/library/SafetyFirst2010.pdf> [accessed 17 July 2013].

STEP 5

Sampling refers to the task of selecting households for surveys and interviews. Sampling can be carried out relatively simply for qualitative work, but is usually a more complex matter for surveys, where the number of respondents is much higher.

Sampling is a specialized technical field, and, for further information, we suggest that the reader consults a sampling or statistical manual, examples of which are provided in 'Further reading' at the end of this section.

In Step 5, we introduce some basic concepts that should be useful when deciding how to choose a sample in the field, including advice on:

- **deciding on the sampling population;**
- **deciding on the sample size;**
- **deciding on the sample design;**
- **specifying the sampling frame.**

5.1 Sampling population

Sampling starts with a decision about what is the relevant population for the evaluation. This might be all the people living in an area, specific communities that were the worst affected by disaster, or, more narrowly still, the people who were recipients of interventions. The Contribution to Change approach generally assumes that the methods will be applied across a set of disaster-affected communities (although, if required, it can also be directed solely to aid recipients).

5.2 Sample size

In most cases, the population affected by a disaster and/or by an intervention will be too large for everyone to be included in a survey. A sample is a subset of this population that is of a manageable size. The choice of sample size is an important decision. Too large a sample size would waste limited resources, while too small a sample would affect the utility of the results.

Because the **qualitative household interviews** are intended to be in depth rather than extensive in coverage, they typically work with small numbers of respondents (measured in tens rather than hundreds; see Box 17).

The difficult balance to strike is with the sample size for the **quantitative household survey**. A small sample – of, for example, 100 households – will provide useful information, and descriptive statistics (see Step 7) can be applied to this sample. However, findings cannot be generalized to the whole population, as the sample is not representative.

For many agencies, where funding is limited, smaller samples providing data for descriptive statistics will be the obvious choice. However, if the aim is to be able to generalize the findings, and to be able to do more complicated inferential statistics (see Step 7), then it is necessary to calculate the minimum sample size required.

Box 17 How big a sample?

Many agencies have a rule of thumb to collect data from 10% of the population. In large-scale surveys, this can often lead to many more questionnaires than necessary being used, and it is a waste of resources.

In order to calculate an adequate sample size, one needs to decide on two parameters: confidence level and confidence interval (see Annex 1 for definitions). To calculate a minimum required sample size, we suggest using a confidence level of 95% or 0.95 and a confidence interval of +/–5. With these two values in mind, one can calculate a sample size using online programmes such as www.surveysystem.com/sscalc.htm. For example, for a population of 5,000 households, and assuming a confidence level of 95% and a confidence interval of +/–5, the sample size should be 357.

When sampling, we recommend including 10 per cent additional households as a back-up plan (so, select 10 additional households for every 100 households in the sample). These additional households will be used as reserves in the event that some of the selected samples are not reachable (people are absent or unwilling to take part) and need to be replaced in the sample.

5.3 Sample design

Sample design refers to the way in which samples are specified and selected. Sample designs can range from simple random sampling to a slightly more complex use of cluster samples and stratified samples. The choice should be made depending on the specific context of the Contribution to Change evaluation.

In principle, a selection of households should be chosen at random across the sampling population – everyone should have the same chance of being selected. However, for practical reasons or in order to target the sampling so that specific social groups can be analysed separately, it is usually necessary first to split the sampling population.

A cluster can refer to one community within a population containing many communities. The selection of a certain number of geographical clusters in which sampling is concentrated is often appropriate for humanitarian contexts if villages are very spread out and distances are large. This may be limited by the available resources, but, whenever possible, one should be careful that the selection of clusters is not limited to those communities that are easy to access. Once a choice of clusters has been made, the sampling of households within each of those clusters should be random.

Another sample design option is to split the population into two or more distinct social groups and then randomly sample within those subsets. This is called stratified sampling. The choice of social groups depends on the context of the evaluation, but it might be considered important to split the analysis between households that have been targeted and those that have not been targeted by the intervention. In other situations it may be important to understand the experiences and perspectives of different ethnic groups or people with different livelihood backgrounds, such as fishers and farmers. Stratified sampling is also required if the intention is to focus on intra-household differences by selecting people by gender or age. Stratified sampling is usually necessary in qualitative work (see Box 18).

In very large surveys, it may be possible to have a sample design that includes both clusters and stratified samples, although the costs and staffing involved in this are multiplicd significantly – especially if the aim is to have sample sizes that are statistically significant for each stratum or cluster (in order to undertake inferential statistics).

The information gained from households in multiple clusters or multiple strata may be combined for analysis, as well as each cluster or social group being analysed separately (see Step 7). Separating out sites and social groups can be particularly important if their disaster or intervention experience is likely to be quite different. Where possible, we recommend separating analyses and using these to inform an aggregate analysis (see Step 9).

Other sampling strategies exist, and the sources listed in the 'Further reading' section can provide details of how and why these are used.

Box 18 Sampling for qualitative data collection

Qualitative data collection using semi-structured interviews with households and groups is typically undertaken with much smaller numbers of people than are required for quantitative surveys. This is partly because the process of writing up and coding each interview transcript takes much longer than for a single questionnaire (see Step 8). But it is also because the focus in these techniques is to explore issues in depth with a selection of interviewees, especially to understand the hows and whys behind people's experiences and perspectives. This is quite a different task from seeking to obtain data on characteristics and trends that are representative of the population.

There is no fixed way of calculating sample size for qualitative work, but it is important that a sufficient number of interviews are undertaken so that one can be confident that a range of opinions within the community has been obtained. We would suggest a *minimum* of 20 household interviews per community for a small-scale sampling population of under 500 households, rising to a *minimum* of 50 for sampling populations of 5,000 households or more.

Households should be chosen at random, but, because of the small sample sizes, it is normally essential to use stratified sampling to ensure that representatives of different social groups are included. It is also best that householders selected for group interviews are not from the same households selected for individual household interviews in order to avoid duplication of opinions (as well as to avoid increasing the burden on people's time). This can be achieved by drawing up separate sampling frames for the two interview types.

5.4 Sampling frame

The final requirement in order to undertake sampling is a listing of households within the sampling population – this is what is known as a sampling frame, and it consists of a list of sampling units. Households are the normally expected sampling unit in this evaluation approach (although it is also feasible to focus on individuals, for example to differentiate the evaluation by gender or age). A household may be defined in broad terms as 'a person or group of persons who occupy part or all of a dwelling, and who usually live together and eat from the same kitchen'.

It should be the field supervisor's job to organize and coordinate sampling (working with community leaders or local authorities if necessary and/or appropriate). Ideally, the field team will have access to lists of households within the relevant population from which to undertake random sampling. In practice, acquiring this information can be difficult or time-consuming and it is important to commence the process of acquiring this information well in advance of the planned fieldwork – for example, during the preliminary investigations (Step 1). This can be the case even for lists of the beneficiaries of interventions. In other cases, people and/or households will have identity cards, which can be used to construct the list of households.

In cases where full lists are not available or cannot be compiled, ad hoc methods through which to develop a sampling frame may be required. These are unlikely to provide a perfectly random sample but can be designed to be 'good enough' for the purposes of the evaluation (see 'Example from the field 6').

Example from the field 6: Selection using community mapping

In the pilots, we found that community mapping can be a convenient selection aid (see Step 3). After drawing a map of the village and roughly indicating the distribution of households, the team divided the map into a number of sections (i.e. clusters). Each field researcher was then assigned to work in specific sectors and visit a random selection of households within each. When sampling in this way, it is important to ensure that the participants assisting with the mapping come from different geographical parts of the community, to ensure that all neighbourhoods are included.

Householders' names should not appear in the final outputs of the evaluation. However, lists of names are likely to be needed through the data collection stage in order to keep track of progress and coordinate the coding of households. These should be kept securely and destroyed when no longer required.

To preserve anonymity and help with data management, one can devise a code system that assigns individual identifiers to specific households, for example A22 (A identifies the community and 22 the household number in this cluster). This code needs to be shared with all the field researchers in order to be recorded on questionnaire sheets and interview documents.

Further reading

On sampling methods

Bamberger, M., Rugh, J. and Mabry, L. (2012) 'Sampling', chapter 15 in *RealWorld Evaluation: Working under Budget, Time, Data, and Political Constraints*, 2nd edn, Thousand Oaks, CA: Sage Publications.

Levy, P.S. and Lemeshow, S. (1999) *Sampling of Populations: Methods and Applications*, New York, NY: John Wiley & Sons, Wiley-Interscience Publications.

STEP 6

Once the sampling strategies have been devised, field data collection can commence. Because this approach relies on data collection methods that should be familiar to most evaluation teams, here we provide only summary details of guidelines for the field data collection process. Readers are recommended to consult the methodology sources in Annex 2 for further details on how to work in the field using questionnaire surveys, semi-structured interviews, and group exercises.

All data must be collected on the basis of informed consent and following the ethical principles described in Step 4.

This section covers how to:

- **plan the fieldwork timing and logistics;**
- **provide supervision in the field and ensure quality control;**
- **conduct questionnaire surveys;**
- **conduct semi-structured interviews;**
- **write up qualitative data.**

6.1 Planning fieldwork

The main field data collection should start as soon as possible after the training to minimize the risk that field investigators forget what they have learned. A realistic fieldwork schedule should be planned, taking into account the best times of day for meeting community members as well as the time and staffing required to conduct the work.

- The community survey can be implemented by one person in the quantitative team, perhaps a senior member as the respondents will often be community leaders. The questionnaire should be designed to take between 45 and 60 minutes.

- Each household questionnaire can be conducted by one or two field investigators. It may be a good idea to start by working in pairs until the investigators have become accustomed to the work. Working in pairs may also be advisable if there are any concerns about personal safety. The questionnaire should take between 45 and 60 minutes.

- Key informant interviews can be undertaken by one experienced investigator, although they often involve more than one respondent. However, it is a good idea for all the qualitative field investigators to be present at these (they also then have the opportunity to meet with community leaders). These interviews should take between 45 and 60 minutes.

- The household interviews can be conducted by one or two field investigators. Again, it may be a good idea to work in pairs until the investigators have become accustomed to the work, or if there are any concerns over personal safety. The interviews should take between 45 and 60 minutes.

- Group interviews require two or three people to ask questions, facilitate discussion, and take notes. These interviews are likely to require 60 to 90 minutes.

- Group exercises typically require two or more members of the team. The time required varies according to the method, but timelines and mapping exercises typically take 45 to 60 minutes.

Note that the time required for data collection (as well as data processing) may be reduced by the use of electronic technologies in the field (see Box 19).

Box 19 Use of advanced technologies

Electronic data collection

Handheld mobile devices are increasingly being used for data collection, especially for questionnaire surveys, and there is now a range of software programs available for this purpose. Handheld devices allow the field investigator to enter the data electronically, reducing the time needed for data entry. They provide a means to undertake rapid validation checks, which means that inconsistent responses can be checked even during the interview. Assuming internet access is available, electronically collected data can be transferred to a central database at the end of each field day, allowing for continuous checks and feedback. The preparation for a computer-assisted survey can be more complicated than for a paper survey, but this is balanced by the substantial time gained during the analysis phase. However, use of these technologies in the field does require a certain level of technical support and appropriate back-up procedures in case of equipment failure (including battery failure).

Global positioning system equipment

Handheld global positioning system (GPS) equipment can also be an asset in the field. GPS devices use satellite signals to determine precise locations in latitude–longitude coordinates. This assists with the tasks of identifying and locating households, both in order to generate sampling frames and to locate selected households once the interviews commence. The GPS unit can also be used as a quality control device to make sure that the interviewer actually visited the household.

6.2 Supervision and quality control

Adequate supervision and monitoring of fieldwork are essential and should be undertaken in the field by senior members of the evaluation team. Intensive support to field investigators is especially important in the early stages of fieldwork. In the early stages, each of the field investigators should be observed while conducting one or more interviews. Careful monitoring is critical for the survey methodologies, which rely on standardized and consistent application of questionnaires. The completed questionnaires should be checked on a daily basis and any mistakes in data entry promptly corrected. Many agencies now recommend, in addition, that quality control teams should be engaged in evaluations (see Box 20).

Box 20 Quality control personnel

Where possible, there should be separate dedicated quality control personnel. They should visit the communities after the field team has left and interview a random selection of households (10%) with a short questionnaire. This is to check whether the interview was done properly, with respect for the respondents and according to both quality and ethical standards. Ideally, an independent third party monitoring the procedures should be in place for quality assurance.

6.3 Conducting questionnaire surveys

Those conducting questionnaires follow the standard procedure laid out in the survey forms. The interview should always commence with the informed consent protocol.

Note that for the community survey it may be necessary or preferable to have more than one respondent to cover all the questions. This is because some respondents may not know the answers to some questions. It may also be better to collect different views and triangulate results.

6.4 Conducting semi-structured interviews

For semi-structured interviews the field process is more flexible. Although the question schedule has pre-selected questions, the interviewer should also be responsive to what is said by the interviewee(s) and ask additional questions for clarification, further explanation, or to probe further on key things they say.

Group interviews are likely to require more forethought and skills in terms of facilitation (see Box 21). Interviewers should try to encourage all the people present to speak and offer their perspectives during the meeting. If necessary, they should directly ask individuals who appear to have something to say but are not ready to interject.

Box 21 Group interview tips

Group meetings need careful planning and attention to detail before people start assembling. For example, if recording group meetings, try to get people to sit close together and near the microphone.

Group interviews need to be well staffed – they need a question-asker or facilitator, a note-taker, and perhaps an extra note-taker when the group conversation becomes complicated. Roles can be swapped if arranged beforehand.

It is generally good practice to provide refreshments for groups.

Group interviews tend to work best if only the selected participants are present. However, in practice this is often very difficult to ensure. They can work well indoors, because other people are generally less likely to intrude into a room.

It can be opportunistic to piggyback group interviews onto existing planned community meetings, but there are limits to this opportunism. Be aware that this implies less control over numbers, sample type, and process – if the meetings have an established chair, then that person may tend to dominate.

Recording of interviews is preferable, but in some cases this is not possible (or people may not wish to be recorded) and the material has to be based on notes written at the time of the interview. In this case it is important to take notes that carefully match what people say – it will be necessary to check these rapidly written notes for readability and comprehensiveness immediately after the interview.

If interviewers are intending to use a recorder, they should check before the start of the interview whether participants are comfortable with a recording device. They should explain that this will make the task easier, and assure participants that the recording will not be shared with other people – it is solely to make sure that the data are complete. If anything is particularly sensitive, the machine can always be switched off for a while. If participants agree, the interviewer can also take some basic notes on paper to cover the main points people make (in case the recording fails, and to help in formulating questions).

6.5 Writing up qualitative data

The aim of qualitative fieldwork is to produce interview material that is as close as possible to what was actually expressed by the research participants. Whether based on notes or transcriptions, the output of qualitative data collection is a set of documents representing the dialogue between the field investigator and the participants. It is therefore important not to paraphrase or summarize, and to include the interviewer's questions.

There is no fixed way to present these documents, but the following are recommended guidelines:

* Use a standardized format.

* Electronic filenames should indicate site and interview type (and include a unique ID code, if it is a household interview).

* At the start of the document, insert again the site, the type of interview, and the respondent's ID (if a household).

* Under each main question, write whatever people have said – preferably just as they said it. Separate this into short paragraphs.

* Provide additional detail where required to aid understanding of what the person has said; for example, where something is difficult to understand from the respondent's own words, add a note of explanation in square brackets.

As part of the training for the research team, it is useful to ask field researchers to transcribe practice interviews so that the supervisor has a chance to comment on the conduct of interviews and how they are written up. Translation may also need to be considered (see Box 22).

Box 22 A note on translation

Bear in mind that the translation of interview transcripts from the local language can be a major cost. A single transcript can run to several pages. Translation of these data may not be required, depending on who is doing the analysis and what language they can work in. If required, it is vitally important that the translations are of high quality and exactly match the original statements made by interviewees.

PART THREE

ANALYSIS AND WRITE-UP

Part Three of the guide provides a recommended methodology for analysis and write-up of the data collected using the tools described in Part Two. It presents five additional steps. They provide guidance on preliminary steps for processing quantitative and qualitative data, followed by guidelines for compilation of results and a combined thematic analysis using both sources of evidence. The approach presented in the guide recommends that the analysis is broken down initially into themes that represent sectors of impact or intervention.

This is followed by detailed guidance on how to develop both sectoral and general conclusions for the evaluation. This includes a method for producing a series of Contribution to Change statements as a shorthand way of conveying the findings. The final step provides brief recommendations on how to present the evaluation in a final report.

http://dx.doi.org/10.3362/9781780448114.003

Overall analysis process

The aim of the analysis is to understand how people's lives changed as a result of the disaster impact, the extent to which they have recovered, and the role of external interventions in that recovery.

The approach assumes that there will be a multidimensional analysis of people's lives, trying to look at change that people experienced in terms of economic livelihood, shelter, and other aspects of well-being (such as health and education).

Although the focus is on the disaster event and its implications, it is crucial that these are not viewed in isolation. In order to understand contribution, it is also necessary to analyse the wider context of post-disaster intervention, including other 'shocks' and challenges faced by communities as they set about the recovery process (see Step 1, Box 9).

The task of analysis for Contribution to Change begins with the initial processing of data to generate preliminary results, followed by a structured analysis building on the results, and culminating in a set of conclusions – all of which should be reflected in the final evaluation report.

Table 3 indicates the steps required for analysis and write-up. These steps, 7 to 11, are described in detail in the remainder of Part Three.

Table 3 Steps in analysis and reporting

Step 7	Preliminary analysis – quantitative	See pages 67–73
Step 8	Preliminary analysis – qualitative	See pages 74–77
Step 9	Developing a narrative of evidence and change	See pages 78–85
Step 10	Conclusions: Contribution to Change	See pages 86–93
Step 11	Finalization and use of the report	See pages 94–95

STEP 7

PRELIMINARY ANALYSIS OF QUANTITATIVE DATA

This section concentrates on the initial steps in the analysis of quantitative data. A series of preparatory tasks are first required in order to transfer data into a form that can be analysed. Following these, work can commence on understanding what each data set reveals.

This step includes advice on how to:

- **enter the data into an electronic format;**
- **clean the data set;**
- **undertake statistical analysis of the data.**

7.1 Data entry

After careful checking and editing of questionnaires so that they are correctly completed (see Step 6), the data should be entered into an electronic format. There are a number of suitable data entry and analysis programs available, capable of handling varying degrees of statistical complexity, among them Microsoft Excel, Sphinx, Epi Info, SPSS Statistics and Stata.

When choosing which data entry program to use, it is important to make sure that the data entry clerks and the programmer have previous experience in using the software and are confident handling the chosen program. It is also important that the data entry clerks receive training on the design of the questionnaire to fully understand the questions and therefore the type of responses and anticipated errors. The training should involve entering data from real, completed questionnaires; these are then re-entered when the data entry commences.

Data entry can be conducted parallel to fieldwork so that any queries that need to be addressed to survey participants can be resolved while field teams are on-site.

7.2 Data cleaning

Data cleaning is the process of detecting and correcting (or removing) corrupt, incomplete, inaccurate, or irrelevant records from the database. Data entry packages should have a command that automatically checks for these errors.

Data errors can occur when the information contained in the hard-copy questionnaire is inconsistent or incorrect. Two examples of this are set out below:

- **Blanks:** this happens when a variable is blank but should not be. In some cases the blank answer can be reliably inferred from other answers. In other cases nothing can be done, resulting in a missing value for this variable. If a variable or a questionnaire has many missing values, it should be disregarded.

- **Skip errors:** this happens when a variable has been filled when it should not have been (i.e. it should have been skipped). In most cases this can be corrected by assessing the other answers, in particular the entry for the question that should have triggered the skip.

Inconsistencies may also be caused by user entry errors, or by corruption of electronic data in transmission or storage.

Statistical methods can also be used to aid data cleaning. By analysing the data using the values of mean, standard deviation, range, or clustering algorithms, it is possible for an expert to find values that are unexpected and likely to be wrong. For example, if it is suspected that one interviewer is filling in false data, a check on that interviewer's data using statistical methods can reveal if this is the case. Although the correction of such data is difficult since the true value is not known, it can be resolved by setting the values to an average or to another statistical value.

7.3 Statistical analysis

The prime objectives of statistical analysis for the quantitative data are to obtain an understanding of the longitudinal changes in household welfare and resources over time, as well as information across the study population on the role of interventions.

The data analyst should be chosen carefully. It should be someone very familiar with the goals of the evaluation, and ideally involved from the design phase. The analyst is crucial, as his or her judgement and choices will shape how the results from the surveys are taken forward in the main analysis (Step 9).

Data analysis techniques include simple descriptive statistics and inferential statistics:

- Descriptive statistics present measures of central tendency (averages – mean, median, and mode) and measures of variability about the average (range and standard deviation). These give the reader a picture of the data collected.

- Inferential statistics include statistical tests. These enable us to make deductions from the data collected, to test hypotheses, and to relate findings from the sample to the wider population. Examples of inferential statistics include correlation, simple regression, and multivariate analysis.

To reduce the complexity of the approach, and because often users are likely to be working with relatively small and simple data sets, we concentrate here mainly on descriptive statistics. However, the use of inferential statistics strengthens the ability to draw conclusions about change and contribution from the survey data, and should be considered if the appropriate data sets and skills are available. Some useful sources of information on inferential statistics are provided in Annex 2.

Descriptive statistics usually aim to describe basic information on the distribution, the central tendency, and the dispersion of the variables of interest (see Box 23). This information is produced using one of the software packages referred to in 7.1 'Data entry', and is typically displayed using tables and/or graphs. Because of the focus of this approach on change over time, one key aspect of interest is the change in key statistics over time – e.g. the percentage change in the mean between T_{-1}, T_{+1} and T_{+2}.

Examples of the use of descriptive statistics are provided at the end of this section.

Box 23 Descriptive statistics – definitions

The **distribution** indicates the frequency with which individual values or ranges of values occur for a specific variable. Distributions may also be displayed using percentages.

The **central tendency** of a distribution is an estimate of the centre of a distribution of values. There are three major types of estimates of central tendency: the mean, the median, and the mode. The mean or average is probably the most commonly used method of describing central tendency. The median, however, is often used for a variable such as income because it is less sensitive to outliers at the extremes of the range of values.

Dispersion refers to the spread of the values around the central tendency. There are two common measures of dispersion: the range and the standard deviation. The standard deviation is a more accurate and detailed estimate of dispersion because an outlier can greatly exaggerate the range. The standard deviation measures the average distance of a numerical variable (see Box 24) from the mean of that variable, and thus provides a measure of the dispersion in the distribution of the variable.

When undertaking and presenting statistical analysis using the survey data, there are a number of key points that have to be considered:

- In multi-site/cluster surveys (see Step 5), a decision has to be made on whether to calculate statistics separately for the different sites; this depends largely on the evaluation design. For some studies this may be of little value. In an evaluation that covers distinct sites with different experiences of impact and intervention, statistics should initially be separated for the specific sites. Nevertheless, it will also be important to provide statistics that combine sites.

- With stratified samples (see Step 5), it may be important for some variables to be tabulated separately for subgroups: for example, recipients and non-recipients of the various kinds of interventions.

- An important distinction to make when displaying results is whether the results are percentages of households or percentages of people. In many cases, these will give different results. For instance, in many countries, better-educated individuals have relatively small families. This implies that the proportion of the population living in households with well-educated heads is smaller than the proportion of households that have a well-educated head.

- It is important also to distinguish between two types of variables: categorical and numerical (see Box 24). Categorical variables are not numbers per se, but codes that describe categories or types. Examples are dwelling characteristics, gender, or marital status. Numerical variables are by their very nature values, such as the number of rooms in a dwelling or the amount of income earned.

Box 24 Numerical and categorical variables

Most numerical variables could be transformed into categorical ones. For instance, the age of the respondent can be collected as a continuous numerical value (say from 0 to 100); however, when deciding how to display the results in a table, one can decide to group responses by age groups (showing the percentage of the population between 0 and 5, 6 and 15, etc.). It is worth noting that the reverse is not true for a categorical variable, i.e. it is not possible to transform a categorical variable into a continuous numerical one. While this might sound like simple common sense, it is important to be aware that the type of variable collected affects the type of results you can display. For instance, if the information on age of the respondent is collected as a numerical variable, the statistics that can be produced include both distribution (frequency) and mean. If the information is collected as age groups, only distribution can be employed (information on the mean would be misleading, as it would show only the mean of the categories used).

Further reading

On use of descriptive statistics

Blaikie, N. (2003) *Analyzing Quantitative Data: From Description to Explanation*, London: Sage Publications.

Taylor-Powell, E. (1996) *Analyzing Quantitative Data*, Madison, WI: University of Wisconsin Cooperative Extension Publications. <http://learningstore.uwex.edu/assets/pdfs/g3658-6.pdf> [accessed 17 July 2013].

Examples of the use of descriptive statistics

For illustration, the following examples relate to a small sample of households in a village affected by flooding.

The chart below shows the distribution of the number of plots that a household was cultivating before a flood, the number of plots lost in the flood (crops destroyed and degradation of topsoil), and the number of plots cultivated at the time of the survey. (The numbers on the horizontal axis refer to the household identifier, i.e. household 1, household 2, etc., and the number on the vertical axis to the number of plots.)

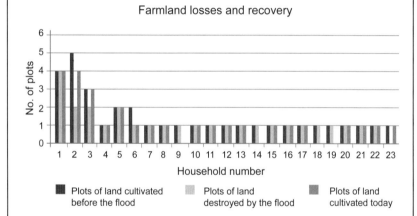

Some figures of interest that could be derived from this data are that:

- 22 of 23 households surveyed reported losses (96%)
- 19 of 23 reported a full loss (83%)
- 16 households reported full recovery (70%)
- 6 households reported partial or no recovery (26%).

The table below compares the level of debt before the flood with subsequent levels of debt.

Money owed at T_{-1}	Money owed at T_{+1}	Money owed at T_{+2}
Mean average		
80,312	300,225	210,442
Standard deviation		
5,325	35,000	18,893
Percentage change in the mean relative to T_{-1}		
–	274%	162%

This table shows that, on average, the levels of debt increased after the floods. The average level of debt increased after the floods from 80,312 to 300,225 (i.e. by 274% – in other words, debt levels were more than tripled after the floods). At the time of the survey, debt levels had decreased to 210,442, showing a partial recovery – although they were still much higher in comparison to debt levels at T_{-1}.

The standard deviation statistics also provide information. At T_{-1}, standard deviation is relatively lower than at T_{+1} or T_{+2}. This means that at T_{+1} and T_{+2} there are fewer households that are close to the mean value (dispersion is higher). In other words, there is a larger difference between the debt levels of different households. This may be because some households were more affected by the floods (and needed to acquire more debt) than others.

Note that with these descriptive statistics it is not possible to establish causality – we cannot be certain that it was the floods that caused changes in levels or differences in debt. However, in combination with other sources of information they do contribute to the evidence about impact and recovery.

STEP 8

PRELIMINARY ANALYSIS OF QUALITATIVE DATA

The tasks required for the preliminary analysis of qualitative data consist of initial data checks followed by a process of coding and collation. Coding is the principal way in which the body of qualitative data from different interview sources can be organized for detailed analysis.

This section covers how to:

- **undertake qualitative data checks;**

- **code the interview documents;**

- **collate information on the coded topics.**

8.1 Qualitative data checks

Before starting to analyse the notes or transcripts from semi-structured interviews (and the notes from any group exercises), it is important to carry out the following data checks:

- Check the labelling of documents to ensure that households can be identified (and cross-referenced with any quantitative data for the same households).

- Check that the format of documents is consistent.

- Scan the interviews rapidly to get a preliminary knowledge of their content (note down any prominent topics that are emerging which are outside the original question topics).

- Scan the interview data for obvious ambiguities or inconsistencies (e.g. conflicting statements made by the same person) that might require return visits to the interviewee for clarification.

Inconsistencies may simply be the result of note-taking or translation errors, but they commonly also arise directly from the responses people give (this is one of the reasons why interviewers should be prepared to ask follow-up questions and probe a little into the answers people give during the course of a semi-structured interview).

8.2 Coding

Coding aims to draw out key themes from across the qualitative evidence and structure it for analysis. Essentially it entails labelling sections of text (from a single phrase to a whole paragraph) to correspond to one of a set of topics. The same topical codes are applied across all the data sources.

Coding can be undertaken either manually on printouts of the interview documents, or via the use of qualitative analysis software (such as Opencode or the more specialist NVivo). Use of software aids greatly when collating coded items, but it still requires on-screen insertion of codes into documents, and unless the answers are particularly long and detailed or the number of interviews high, this may not be efficient.

We recommend two stages or levels of coding.

The first level of coding should draw on the original question themes used in interviews together with any additional insights into important topics drawn from the preliminary reading of interview documents.

As for the design of tools, we do not provide a blueprint for coding topics because this should be developed specifically to match the case being evaluated. However, the following is one example of possible first-level codes:

- **'Event'** [what happened, the nature of the disaster]

- **'Immediate Impact'** [within 72 hours]

- **'Ongoing Impact'** [longer term]

- **'Coping'** [strategies or actions for surviving during the event – the immediate response]

- **'Response'** [evidence of actions and strategies for recovering after the event – the ongoing response]

- **'Intervention'** [assistance and interventions received from others in the community, from government, or from external agencies]

- **'DRM'** [activities to mitigate and prepare for disaster risk, including information provision]

- **'Other stresses'** [other major shocks, challenges, and changes].

The task is then to go through the documents, coding sections of text that refer to these broad topics. The same part of the document can have overlapping coded sections, but it is not necessary to code all parts of the interview material if some sections are not analytically useful.

Although the coding topics are likely to correspond roughly to the questions asked, do not be restricted to coding just the answers to those corresponding questions – look for relevant information for each topic throughout the document.

Second-level coding examines in more detail sub-topics within this overall structure. These should be based on a re-read of the transcripts, and a listing of relevant sub-topics that could apply to the coded sections.

Sub-topics can be based on different categories of interest (e.g. types of impact, types of activity, sectors of intervention), as well as different aspects of a question (e.g. stated reasons for an action, or perceptions of effectiveness).

In general, we recommend that sub-topics should include reference to specific sectors – such as housing, economic activities, health and hygiene, and food security (coded in relation to impact, recovery, and intervention). This is because the Contribution to Change analysis described in this guide is organized mainly on the basis of sectors (see Steps 9 to 11).

An example of second-level coding applied to sections coded **'Response'** could be the following:

- **'Work'** [employment]
- **'Farming'** [crops, livestock]
- **'Shelter'** [housing, physical assets]
- **'Health'** [health, hygiene, nutrition, stress]
- **'Food'** [food security]
- **'Other'**
- **'Effective'** [perceived effective strategy]
- **'Failed'** [perceived ineffective strategy]
- **'Barriers'** [barriers to recovery].

The code for a segment of text can then be identified as **'Response – Health'**, for example.

Second-level coding can have added levels of complexity where required. For example, a coding scheme for **'Intervention'** could combine types of aid and names of organizations, so that a segment of text is identified as **'Intervention – Housing – NGO1'**. However, it is not recommended to have more than three levels in the coding scheme.

Once a second-level coding scheme has been devised, the coder should go through the sources again, coding to this second level while, at the same time, noting any illustrative quotes from interview transcripts for possible inclusion in the report.

At this stage it is useful for a second analyst to go through a set of clean documents, applying the same coding scheme. This provides an opportunity to check if the coding has been comprehensively and appropriately applied to the data.

8.3 Collation

The final stage in preliminary analysis is to combine and compare information from the different sources on each of the coded topics.

Collation can be done simply by reading and comparing the commonly coded sections of different documents and drawing out key findings. Where there are large numbers of interview documents, however, it is often difficult to do this without physically bringing those coded sections together into a new document. This is where qualitative analysis software becomes especially useful, enabling very rapid presentation of collated sections.

Collating information under the same codes from the different qualitative data sources enables the analyst to look for statements and perspectives that are repeated across the interviews, as well as statements and perspectives that reveal differences in experience or viewpoint. Both the generalizable and the respondent-specific points will be useful in the full analysis (Step 9).

Further reading

On qualitative analysis

Gibson, W.J. and Brown, A. (2009) *Working with Qualitative Data*, London: Sage Publications.
Miles, M.B., Huberman, A.M. and Saldaña, J. (2013) *Qualitative Data Analysis: A Methods Sourcebook*, 3rd edn, Thousand Oaks, CA: Sage Publications.
Shaw, I.F. (1999) *Qualitative Evaluation*, London: Sage Publications.

STEP 9

Following preliminary analyses of data, the next step is to produce two substantial written sections as the main inputs to the evaluation report (Step 11):

- a detailed presentation of the results, combining findings from the quantitative and qualitative data;

- an analytical section covering a series of relevant themes, each drawing on the quantitative and qualitative evidence of recovery and the role of interventions.

This detailed work will provide the evidence and analysis on which conclusions can be made about contribution to change in the step that follows (Step 10). It requires good skills in integrating mixed-method results and drawing out key analytical points in a written form. It is preferable that this task is undertaken by senior team members with experience in this type of analysis.

Step 9 provides guidance on how to:

- **decide on a structure for the results section of the report;**

- **compile and integrate results from the quantitative and qualitative data;**

- **draw on the results to analyse the recovery and intervention.**

9.1 Structure of the results section

This represents the main presentation of evidence. It should be logically structured so that there is a clear distinction between evidence on impacts, on livelihood trajectories, and on interventions (although links can be made between them).

The structure may vary according to the context of the evaluation, but in general we recommend the following basis for organizing the evidence:

- local context (including non-disaster-related issues);

- specific disaster experience (with a summary statement of the types of impact on the community and its members – consider that the impacts of disasters on people's lives can unfold according to different timescales, with some experienced immediately and some in the longer term);

- changes in household livelihoods from T_{-1} (before the disaster) to T_{+1} (shortly after) to T_{+2} (the recovery period) – this should look at different aspects of people's lives and livelihoods, drawing mainly on the quantitative data sets, but also backing this up with references and quotes from the qualitative data;

- patterns of intervention – again, ideally drawing on both quantitative and qualitative data.

In cases where data collection has been undertaken in a small number of distinct sites, it may be useful to present these as separate case studies, with the same structure repeated for each site. For situations where the experience of impact and intervention is much less differentiated between sites, it might be feasible or preferable (e.g. if there are many cluster samples) to provide an account that combines data from across the sites.

9.2 Compilation of the results section

Taking the quantitative evidence first, tables, statistics, and graphs, and their explanations, should be structured within the results section as appropriate, with text that explains and highlights what they show. At this stage expect to be selective – a large amount of data are likely to be available from the surveys and not all can or should be included. It is important not to have too many complex tables in the report, but to include the ones that provide the best insights and understanding. Findings from other tabulations can be presented as summary text.

This should then be combined with qualitative information drawn from the collated topics and sub-topics. Again, it is not necessary to include everything that has been collated in Step 8. If the information does not really provide any insights, it can be omitted. However, it is important to present evidence in as neutral a way as possible, including differing perspectives and conflicting statements between sources. It is useful to refer to how many people expressed the same or a similar view. Quotes from interviews can be used to illustrate the points people make (but they must be anonymous – see Step 11).

Together, the sources of quantitative and qualitative information should form an integrated account of the changes and actions since the disaster event. Some examples are given at the end of this section that show how extracts from an integrated account might be presented.

9.3 Analytical section

The compilation of evidence in the results section then provides the basis for the analytical section, which brings together and discusses the implications of the findings across the sites. This discussion draws out the evidence of and insights into the impact and recovery process and critically examines the role that intervention played.

The recommended approach is to arrange this analytical section by 'sectors' of impact and intervention. This approach makes it easier to draw conclusions about contribution to change in the next step (Step 10). The precise choice of sectors depends again on the scope and focus of the evaluation, but, *as an example*, for a context in which damage to housing and crops is the major sectoral concern, the thematic headings might be:

• housing;

• crops;

• other economic impacts;

• other impacts (e.g. health, WASH, education);

• cross-cutting factors.

Under the sectoral headings (in this case the first four), there would be a discussion of disaster impacts, recovery patterns, and the role of intervention relevant to that sector. This should include any evidence of social differentiation and equity issues in impact, recovery, and receipt of assistance (including gender, age, and other intra-household dimensions), and evidence of any disaster risk-reduction or poverty-reduction activity (i.e. moving beyond the recovery of former states).

Under the 'cross-cutting factors' heading would appear wider factors that affected recovery or shaped intervention, such as:

• other hazards or crises;

• political, economic, social, and environmental changes;

• aspects of governance and decision making;

• any unintended consequences of intervention.

The quality of this analytical section is key in the task of developing and supporting conclusions about contribution to change (Step 10). Although it involves interpretation from results, it is vital that it is approached in a rigorous and balanced way. *As a general principle, points made in the analytical section should be triangulated from more than one source.* This is an important check to help maximize the validity of the analysis.

Some examples are given at the end of this section that show how extracts from an analytical section might be presented.

Examples of the compilation of results

Changes

... The destruction of paddy fields and, in some cases, next year's seeds, which were in storage, was felt in terms of a loss of capital and an increase in indebtedness. The damage to paddy fields translates into a loss of employment as well as personal income, as in most cases the flood removed the possibility of wage labour in others' fields. Few households had savings or capital to fall back on to compensate for these losses.

The effect has put us into huge trouble. I am not a family head who gains regular income or who has various ways for earning money. I'm a labourer and a household head who earns money for daily life. I don't have money in the bank. The last flood caused spending of the little amount of money that I had saved for future life.

(male, 37 years old, household head) ...

... The following chart provides an overview of the changes in labour participation.

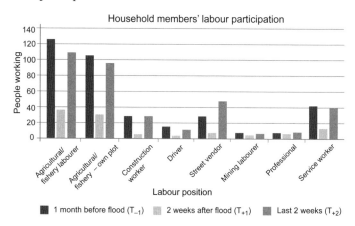

The chart suggests that there have not been major changes in the types of work resulting from the flood. Most people were out of work in the period immediately following the floods, but attempted to return to their original occupations. By the time of the survey, numbers of people working as agricultural labourers or on their own farming plots had been restored to 89% and 94% of their pre-flood levels. The most dramatic change was in the number of street vendors (a 65% increase). Local key informants indicated that this was linked with interventions to promote market gardening ...

Intervention

... Livelihoods assistance in the village mostly took the form of agricultural inputs and livestock, with 67% of respondents indicating that they received assistance of this kind. [Organization A] provided two goats to 40 families, chickens to 15 families and cattle to one family. However, several people complained that the goats and chickens were diseased or not vaccinated, and several of them died. [Organization B] provided seed, and some people also received fertilizer under the same scheme. The amount of seed provided was reportedly not enough to bring beneficiaries up to their previous level. Those survey respondents receiving seed estimated that it compensated 25–60% (mean 36%) of their original acreage.

Seed given by [Organization B] is not enough to recover our paddy cultivation like before. We had to spend our money for more seed paddy and other labour works. We had not gained any profit during the flood and even in the successive cultivation.'
(male, 39 years old, household head)

I got Rs. 20,000/- as compensation for paddy cultivation and six bushels of seed paddy. It's not enough to recover at least my investment again. I spent nearly 100,000/- for my paddy cultivation including fertilizer and labour wages.
(male, 55 years old, household head)

[Organization B] gave seed paddy and cash compensation to paddy farmers at a rate of about two bushels per acre, but only gave it to those who were registered in the Paddy Land Register (holding the deeds to the land). This resulted in several affected households being unable to receive assistance, as the deeds were in other relatives' names, for example: *We got nothing as agriculture assistance ...*

Examples of analytical text

Housing

... Completed brick houses were seen as a significant source of recovery and improvement in general well-being, and even incomplete houses were regarded as at least in some way positive. By the time of the survey, the houses funded by [Organization C] in village A were complete. The gain of a new brick house, with latrine and water tank, was seen as significantly improving quality of life for beneficiaries.

In villages B and C the houses funded by [Organization D] employed local masons, thus also providing employment as well as housing. At the time of the survey, however, most of these houses were not completed, and this was generally reported to be because of insufficient funds (the provision of funding per house was 20% of that provided by [Organization C]). At this stage of recovery, it is difficult to ascertain whether the half-built houses will be positive or negative overall in the long run. Right now, respondents are mostly dissatisfied with the provision of aid which left houses incomplete, but if they are able to complete them themselves in another year's time, they may feel there has been an overall benefit.

Those who did not receive housing assistance because their houses were relatively undamaged or because they did not have young children were quite likely to say that the distribution of aid was unfair. There is some underlying resentment and sense of inequity in the level of assistance received by some households under the intervention by [Organization C] ...

Other economic impacts

… Almost all respondents experienced the loss of income from the destruction of crops as an increase in indebtedness. Although most households have some assets and capital, this is mostly not in the form of ready cash. Most households live in a debt cycle, where jewellery is pawned at the beginning of each season to purchase seeds and other inputs. The loss of the harvest meant an inability to redeem pawned goods, as profit from the harvest was the only source of cash with which to buy back goods. The loss of crops therefore also meant the overall potential loss of capital and assets, and the removal of the principal strategy of business investment. The long-term impact of the floods' effect on livelihoods is thus seen not only in terms of losing an investment for this year, but also in taking away the capacity for further investment. The availability of cash was an important livelihood need after the flood that remained unaddressed by post-disaster interventions.

Although the number of surveyed households needing loans did not change significantly, the average value of money owed greatly increased after the floods and in many cases debt levels remain higher than before (in village A, nearly three times as high). Although indebtedness for individual households is related to many factors other than the impacts of the flood, comparison of the mean and modes for levels of debt at T_{-1} and T_{+2} suggest that flood-related debt remains a significant livelihood impact across the communities, an observation that was strongly backed up by household interviews …

STEP 10

CONCLUSIONS: CONTRIBUTION TO CHANGE

The desired end product of the analysis is a conclusion about the contribution to change arising from post-disaster intervention. This should be the concluding section of the report, bringing together insights from the preceding thematic analyses.

As well as providing a written discussion, this can include a set of robust but interpretative statements about contribution – assessing qualitatively to what extent the intervention actions have made a difference.

This step covers how to:

- **draw conclusions about the levels of recovery and the reasons why those levels of change have been achieved in each key sector;**

- **generate a set of 'contribution statements' for each key sector;**

- **discuss contribution to change in general terms, including general factors that have shaped the effectiveness of intervention.**

10.1 Sectoral conclusions

Building on the evidence and analysis presented in Step 9, the recommended first step in this final part of the evaluation is to write brief conclusions about recovery for each key sector. In most cases the number of sectors for which this is carried out will be limited to the major sectors already identified as being of particular importance in the context of the evaluation (see 9.3 'Analytical section').

Each of these sectoral conclusions should use the preceding evidence to:

- summarize the level of recovery – the extent to which people's assets, needs, or access to services relating to this sector have been restored or improved since the disaster event;

- explain what accounts for this level (or lack) of progress, noting the relative importance of people's own actions, community-based activities, and external interventions.

The aim here is to make robust conclusions about the progress of recovery (compared with what is required), and to see how the contribution that interventions have made to what has been achieved compares with the efforts of the people and communities themselves.

In reality, of course, there are likely to be varying experiences of both recovery and intervention both within and between the communities sampled for the evaluation. Although the text here should aim to make generalized points where possible, it may also be important to highlight where there are major differences in experience.

10.2 Contribution statements

In order to provide a simpler means of conveying conclusions about contribution to change, we present here a method through which to derive Contribution to Change statements. These can be applied to each of the key sectors in turn, and presented alongside the text produced in 10.1 'Sectoral conclusions'. (In some cases it may be feasible to generate these statements about recovery in general – i.e. across all aspects of people's lives – but it is more difficult to provide a simple method for this, partly because it requires a basis on which to weigh up the relative importance of the different sectors.)

As described in Part One, the ultimate purpose of contribution statements is to interpret the *positive* contribution that intervention has made towards building the recovery that is *needed*. This is what we refer to as 'contribution to change'.

A contribution statement is therefore based on:

A: the level of recovery achieved in relation to what is required;

B: the contribution of the intervention to the recovery that has been achieved;

C: the combination of A and B to reveal the contribution to change.

For each of **A**, **B**, and **C**, the task is to decide which category, from 'high' to 'low', applies for the sector. Note that the methods for deriving a category for **B**, and of combining **A** and **B** to create a category for **C**, are slightly complicated processes. However, a series of tables and diagrams are provided at the end of this section to guide the reader through them.

For stage **A** and stage **B**, the method involves assigning one of three categories (high, medium, or low). For stage **C**, two intermediary categories are provided to enable a wider range of Contribution to Change outcomes to be generated.

The product of these three stages is a series of complementary **contribution statements** that apply to each of the key sectors. Three examples of sets of contribution statements are shown in Box 25.

Box 25 Examples of sets of contribution statements

Level of recovery achieved – LOW
Contribution of intervention to recovery achieved – MEDIUM
Contribution to change – MEDIUM–LOW

Level of recovery achieved – MEDIUM
Contribution of intervention to recovery achieved – HIGH
Contribution to change – MEDIUM–HIGH

Level of recovery achieved – HIGH
Contribution of intervention to recovery achieved – LOW
Contribution to change – LOW

The Contribution to Change statements are, in effect, a shorthand device with which to interpret in simple terms the findings of the evaluation. However, this does not mean that the method can be approached casually. The contribution statements need to be based *robustly* on a clear trail of evidence presented in the report under the thematic narrative (Step 9) and summarized in the conclusion (see 10.1 'Sectoral conclusions').

10.3 General conclusions

It is important that the conclusion does not end with the sectoral contribution statements. It is recommended that the final part of the conclusion should attempt to draw more general points about the progress of recovery in the population and the factors that have shaped this. The data collection methods employed in the Contribution to Change approach are intended to yield a rich source of information not limited solely to levels and causes of recovery in specific sectors.

A discussion should be provided that:

• reviews overall patterns of recovery, and the relative importance in this of people's own actions and community-based activities compared with external interventions;

- discusses the main reasons why change has or has not been achieved;

- raises any additional economic, social, cultural, political, or environmental factors that have strongly shaped the effectiveness of the interventions in bringing about recovery;

- identifies any negative consequences or unintended impacts of interventions (in effect, these can be thought of as contributions to negative change);

- identifies whether the interventions themselves have raised issues of fairness in the social distribution of aid;

- identifies whether the interventions have created or affected (positively or negatively) issues of equity and power relations within the communities or within households (e.g. according to gender or age).

Some of these wider issues may also be investigated in depth through parallel types of evaluation (see Part One).

How to generate Contribution to Change statements

Stage A: Level of recovery achieved

Assign a category (high, medium, or low) for the sector.

	High	Medium	Low
Stage A: Level of recovery achieved **SECTOR** .... **HIGH?** **MEDIUM?** **LOW?**	**Ongoing disaster impacts do not appear to be being experienced now by most of the affected households.** Relevant aspects of the livelihoods and well-being of the affected households have been almost restored, fully restored, or improved.	**Some ongoing disaster impacts are still being experienced by most of the affected households.** Although some recovery has been made, relevant aspects of the livelihoods and well-being still show clear signs of impact.	**Ongoing disaster impacts are still seriously affecting most of the affected households.** There has been little or no recovery in relevant aspects of the livelihoods and well-being of affected households.

Note 1: '**most**' means two-thirds or more of households.
Note 2: '**affected households**' refers to households that experienced losses or disruption *in the sector of interest*.
Note 3: '**relevant aspects**' refers to the sector of interest (e.g. crop harvests, cash income for the agriculture sector).

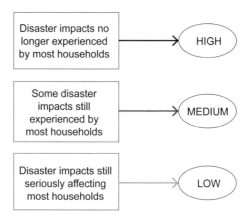

Stage B: Contribution to recovery achieved

Assign a category (high, medium, or low) for the sector.

	High	Medium	Low
Stage B: Contribution to recovery achieved SECTOR .... HIGH? MEDIUM? LOW?	The intervention appears to have had a major effect on any positive change experienced in this sector. The intervention has benefited most (two-thirds or more) of the disaster-affected households in the community. AND It is regarded positively by most households. OR* There is a general perception and/or evidence that it has had a major effect in bringing about change. OR* It is unlikely that the change would have been achieved without the intervention.	The intervention appears to have made some significant contribution to any positive change achieved in this sector. The intervention has benefited a significant proportion (one- to two-thirds) of the disaster-affected households in the community. AND It is regarded as bringing at least some benefit. OR* There is a general perception and/or evidence that it has had at least a minor effect in bringing about change.	It is unlikely that the intervention has had a positive effect in this sector. The intervention has benefited a small proportion (less than one-third) of the disaster-affected households in the community. OR* There is a general perception and/or evidence that it has not been effective in bringing about change. OR* It is likely that the change would have been achieved regardless of the intervention.

Note 4: We focus on 'positive effect' here because intervention can also create negative consequences (see 10.3 'General conclusions').

Note 5: *We include alternative ways of assigning the category of contribution to recovery achieved in order to broaden the types of evidence that can be used to make this judgement. In cases of ambiguity, the team has to decide which of the alternative statements in the different columns most closely matches the evidence.

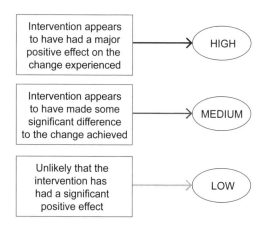

Stage C: Contribution to change

Combine stages A and B to undertake stage C, as shown here.

	High	Medium–high	Medium	Medium–low	Low
Stage C: Contribution to change **SECTOR** .... **HIGH?** **MEDIUM–HIGH?** **MEDIUM?** **MEDIUM–LOW?** **LOW?**	**Combination of:** High in A + High in B	**Combination of:** Medium in A + High in B	**Combination of:** High in A + Medium in B OR Medium in A + Medium in B	**Combination of:** Low in A + High in B OR Low in A + Medium in B	**Combination of:** High in A + Low in B OR Medium in A + Low in B OR Low in A + Low in B

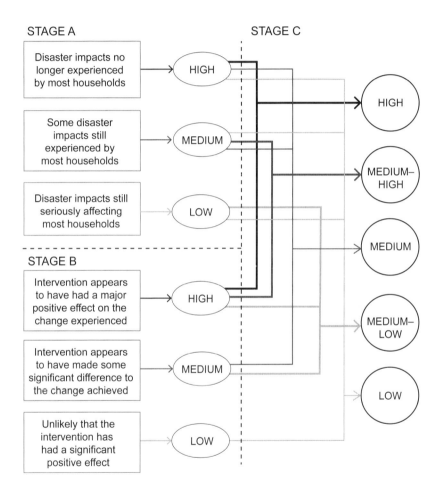

STEP 11

FINALIZATION AND USE OF THE REPORT

The final step is the compilation of a report. The report is a resource available to agencies against which they can gauge the effectiveness of external interventions. Drawing on the previous two sections (Step 9 and Step 10), we suggest that a typical content for a Contribution to Change evaluation report is as follows:

- Introduction: briefly describes the disaster event and the purpose of the evaluation and its objectives;

- Methods: outlines the ideas behind the approach and the data collection and analysis methods;

- Results: presents the evidence (as suggested in 9.2 'Compilation of the results section');

- Analysis: discusses the results (as suggested in 9.3 'Analytical section');

- Conclusions: sets out concluding points on Contribution to Change by sector (linking 10.1 'Sectoral conclusions' and 10.2 'Contribution statements') and overall (10.3 'General conclusions').

The report relies on interpretation and judgements made on the basis of a fairly complex body of evidence. If the conclusions are to be credible then this process needs to be transparent. It is therefore important to ensure that the presentation of evidence in the results section of the report is adequate, readily understandable, and presented consistently. It should be clear to the reader what the sources of information (data sources) are for the different evidence that is presented.

However, it is also important that the outputs of the work are anonymized. That means that the names of people who contributed their information and perspectives to the evaluation should not appear in the evaluation report and other products. It also means that neutral terms should be used to refer to the role of key informants, so that individuals cannot be identified by their job titles.

As discussed in Part One, the Contribution to Change approach brings important insights, but it is just one form of evaluation. Other approaches are likely to be needed to focus on operations and deliverables. Although equity and gender considerations could be revealed through the analysis presented here, full assessment of these dimensions should perhaps also be undertaken through a more targeted type of evaluation.

The final report presents Contribution to Change findings on a specific intervention context, but its value can be broader than this. When grounded in thorough and thoughtful analysis, it presents an opportunity for learning more widely about the effectiveness and relative importance of intervention practices in bringing about positive change in the lives of those affected by disaster.

ANNEXES

ANNEX 1

Glossary

This glossary presents explanations of terms as they are used in the guide. It has been adapted from a number of terminology sources, including the Organisation for Economic Co-operation and Development's (OECD's) *Glossary of Key Terms in Evaluation and Results Based Management* (www.oecd.org/dac/2754804.pdf) and the United Nations International Strategy for Disaster Reduction's (UNISDR's) 'Terminology on disaster risk reduction' (www.unisdr.org/we/inform/terminology).

Attribution The ascription of a causal link between observed changes and a specific intervention.

Baseline The data collected at the start of an intervention in order to do a comparison at the end of the intervention to measure changes that may or may not have occurred.

Beneficiaries The individuals, groups, or organizations, whether targeted or not, that benefit, directly or indirectly, from the intervention.

Bias An effect that undermines the representativeness of a statistical result by systematically distorting it, as distinct from a random error which may distort on any one occasion but balances out on average.

Cluster sampling When the basic sampling unit in the population is to be found in groups or clusters, e.g. households in villages, the sampling is sometimes carried out by selecting a sample of clusters and observing members within each selected cluster.

Coding (qualitative) A system for labelling sections of text according to a set of themes, applied across different qualitative data sources so that information on the same theme can be compared and collated.

Coding (surveys) Assigning a system of codes (usually in the form of letters and numerals) for each category of each variable in a survey.

Confidence interval Also called the margin of error, this is an estimated range of values usually expressed as a plus or minus figure. For example, using a confidence interval of +/−4, if 47% of the sample picks an answer there is confidence that, had the same question been asked in the whole population, between 43% (47 minus 4) and 51% (47 plus 4) would have had the same answer.

Confidence level   The confidence level is expressed as a percentage (90%, 95%, or 99%) and represents how often the true percentage of the population with the same answer lies within the confidence interval.

Contribution   The extent to which external intervention can be said to have contributed to observed changes.

Control group   A group of subjects closely resembling the group receiving the intervention and thereby serving as a comparison group when the effect of the intervention is evaluated.

Descriptive statistics   Statistical procedures used for describing the characteristics of a data set.

Disaster   A serious disruption of the functioning of a community or a society involving widespread human, material, economic, or environmental losses and impacts, which exceeds the ability of the affected community or society to cope using its own resources.

Disaster risk reduction   The concept and practice of reducing disaster risks through systematic efforts to analyse and manage the causal factors of disasters.

Effectiveness   A measure of the extent to which an aid activity attains its objectives.

Efficiency   A measure of the extent to which aid uses the least costly resources possible in order to achieve the desired results.

Endline   The data collected at the end of an intervention and compared with the baseline.

Evaluation   Systematic collection of data on project planning and implementation, in order to design, monitor, and critically assess its efficiency, effectiveness, impact, sustainability, replicability, and/or the relevance of its objectives.

Impact   The positive and negative changes produced by an intervention, directly or indirectly, intended or unintended.

Indicator   Quantitative or qualitative factor or variable that provides a simple and reliable means to measure achievement, to reflect the changes connected to an intervention, or to help assess the performance of a development actor.

Inferential statistics   Statistical techniques for drawing inferences or conclusions about the characteristics of a population using information from a sample of that population.

Monitoring   A continuous process of collecting and analysing information to compare against planned activities in order to measure progress and to correct or address any problems that may impede the achievement of results.

Multivariate analysis   Statistical procedures for the analysis of data involving more than one type of measurement or observation. It may also mean the procedure where more than one dependent variable is analysed simultaneously with other variables.

Outcomes   The likely or achieved short- and medium-term effects of an intervention's outputs, expressed in terms of change.

Output   The product of the activities that can be directly attributed to the intervention – such as provision of health services or distribution of farming tools.

Qualitative methods   Data collection and analysis that focus on deriving in-depth information about perspectives and experiences.

Quantitative methods   Data collection and analysis that focus on the frequencies of responses to questions through the use of statistics.

Random sampling   A sampling technique in which a selected sampling unit (e.g. a household) is chosen entirely by chance from the sampling population.

Recovery   The restoration, and improvement where appropriate, of facilities, livelihoods, and living conditions of disaster-affected communities.

Relevance   The extent to which the aid activity is suited to the priorities and policies of the target group, recipient, and donor.

Reliability   Consistency or dependability of data and evaluation judgements, with reference to the quality of the instruments, procedures, and analyses used to collect and interpret evaluation data.

Retrospective data collection   Collection of data referring to a previous point or points in time.

Sample size   The number of sampling units that are to be included in the sample.

Sampling   The process of selecting a number of cases from all the cases in a particular group or population.

Sampling frame   The list of the sampling units that is used in the selection of a sample.

Stratified sampling   A sampling design in which the population is divided into subgroups or strata, within each of which sampling is then conducted.

Sustainability   Evaluating whether the benefits of an activity are likely to continue after donor funding has been withdrawn.

Triangulation   The use of multiple sources or types of information, or types of analysis, to verify and substantiate an assessment.

Validity The extent to which the data collection strategies and instruments measure what they are intended to measure.

Variable A quantity or quality that is changeable and measurable.

ANNEX 2

References and further resources

Monitoring and evaluation

Bakewell, O., Adams, J. and Pratt, B. (2004) *Sharpening the Development Process: A Practical Guide to Monitoring and Evaluation*, Oxford: INTRAC.

Bamberger, M., Rugh, J. and Mabry, L. (2012) *RealWorld Evaluation: Working under Budget, Time, Data, and Political Constraints*, 2nd edn, Thousand Oaks, CA: Sage Publications.

Buttenheim, A. (2009) *Impact Evaluation in the Post-disaster Setting: A Conceptual Discussion in the Context of the 2005 Pakistan Earthquake*, 3IE Working Paper 5, Washington, DC: International Initiative for Impact Evaluation.

Cosgrave, J., Ramalingam, B. and Beck, T. (2009) *Real-time Evaluations of Humanitarian Action: An ALNAP Guide*, Pilot Version, London: ALNAP. <www.alnap.org/pool/files/rteguide.pdf> [accessed 17 July 2013].

Gosling, L. and Edwards, M. (2003) *Toolkits: A Practical Guide to Planning, Monitoring, Evaluation and Impact Assessment*, Save the Children Development Manuals, London: Save the Children UK.

Mazurana, D., Benelli, P., Gupta, H. and Walker, P. (2011) *Sex and Age Matter: Improving Humanitarian Response in Emergencies*, Somerville, MA: Feinstein International Center, Tufts University. <http://sites.tufts.edu/feinstein/2011/sex-and-age-matter> [accessed 17 July 2013].

Stufflebeam, D.L. (2004) 'Evaluation design checklist' on the Evaluation Center's Evaluation Checklists [website] <www.wmich.edu/evalctr/checklists/> [accessed 17 July 2013].

Participatory evaluation

Fetterman, D.M. (2000) *Foundations of Empowerment Evaluation*, Thousand Oaks, CA: Sage Publications.

Feuerstein, M.-T. (1986) *Partners in Evaluation: Evaluating Development and Community Programmes with Participants*, London: Macmillan.

Mebrahtu, E. (2004) *Putting Policy into Practice: Participatory Monitoring and Evaluation in Ethiopia*, Oxford: INTRAC.

Impact measurement

Catley, A., Burns, J., Abebe, D. and Suji, O. (2008) *Participatory Impact Assessment: A Guide for Practitioners*, Somerville, MA: Feinstein International Center, Tufts University. <www.preventionweb.net/english/professional/publications/v.php?id=9679> [accessed 17 July 2013].

Gertler, P.J., Martinez, S., Premand, P., Rawlings, L.B. and Vermeersch, C.M.J. (2010) *Impact Evaluation in Practice*, Washington, DC: World Bank. <http://documents.worldbank.org/curated/en/2011/01/13871146/impact-evaluation-practice> [accessed 17 July 2013].

O'Flynn, M. (2010) *Impact Assessment: Understanding and Assessing our Contributions to Change*, M&E Paper 7, Oxford: INTRAC. <www.intrac.org/data/files/resources/695/Impact-Assessment-Understanding-and-Assessing-our-Contributions-to-Change.pdf> [accessed 17 July 2013].

Proudlock, K., Ramalingam, B. and Sandison, P. (2009) 'Improving humanitarian impact assessment: bridging theory and practice', in ALNAP, *8th Review of Humanitarian Action: Performance, Impact and Innovation*, London: ALNAP. <www.alnap.org/pool/files/8rhach2.pdf> [accessed 17 July 2013].

Roche, C. (1999) *Impact Assessment for Development Agencies: Learning to Value Change*, Oxford: Oxfam Publishing.

Scoones, I. (1998) *Sustainable Rural Livelihoods: A Framework for Analysis*, IDS Working Paper 72, Brighton: Institute of Development Studies.

Stern, E., Stame, N., Mayne, J., Forss, K., Davies, R. and Befani, B. (2012) *Broadening the Range of Designs and Methods for Impact Evaluations: Report of a Study Commissioned by the Department for International Development*, Working Paper 38, London: DFID. <www.gov.uk/government/uploads/system/uploads/attachment_data/file/67427/design-method-impact-eval.pdf> [accessed 17 July 2013].

General data collection

Bamberger, M., Rao, V. and Woolcock, M. (2010) *Using Mixed Methods in Monitoring and Evaluation: Experiences from International Development*, Policy Research Working Paper 5245, Washington, DC: World Bank.

Herlihy, J., Jobson, L. and Turner, S. (2012) 'Just tell us what happened to you: autobiographical memory and seeking asylum', *Applied Cognitive Psychology* 26: 661–76. <http://dx.doi.org/10.1002/acp.2852>.

Mertens, D.M. and Wilson, A.T. (2012) *Program Evaluation Theory and Practice: A Comprehensive Guide*, New York, NY: Guilford Press.

Robson, C. (2011) *Real World Research*, 3rd edn, Chichester: John Wiley & Sons.

Quantitative data collection

Blair, J., Czaja, R.F. and Blair, E.A. (2013) *Designing Surveys: A Guide to Decisions and Procedures*, 3rd edn, Thousand Oaks, CA: Sage Publications.

Iarossi, G. (2006) *The Power of Survey Design: A User's Guide for Managing Surveys, Interpreting Results, and Influencing Respondents*, Washington, DC: World Bank.

Osborne, J.W. (2008) *Best Practices in Quantitative Methods*, Thousand Oaks, CA: Sage Publications.

Qualitative data collection

Bamberger, M., Rugh, J. and Mabry, L. (2012) 'Qualitative evaluation approaches', chapter 13 in *RealWorld Evaluation: Working under Budget, Time, Data, and Political Constraints*, 2nd edn, Thousand Oaks, CA: Sage Publications.

Gibson, W.J. and Brown, A. (2009) *Working with Qualitative Data*, London: Sage Publications, pp. 84–126.

Krueger, R.A. and Casey, M.A. (2008) *Focus Groups: A Practical Guide for Applied Research*, 4th edn, Thousand Oaks, CA: Sage Publications.

Patton, M.Q. (2002a) *Qualitative Evaluation & Research Methods*, 3rd edn, Thousand Oaks, CA: Sage Publications, pp. 207–339.
Patton, M.Q. (2002b) 'Qualitative evaluation checklist' on the Evaluation Center's Evaluation Checklists [website] <www.wmich.edu/evalctr/checklists/> [accessed 17 July 2013].

Sampling

Bamberger, M., Rugh, J. and Mabry, L. (2012) 'Sampling', chapter 15 in *RealWorld Evaluation: Working under Budget, Time, Data, and Political Constraints*, 2nd edn, Thousand Oaks, CA: Sage Publications.
Henry, G.T. (1990) *Practical Sampling*, Thousand Oaks, CA: Sage Publications.
Levy, P.S. and Lemeshow, S. (1999) *Sampling of Populations: Methods and Applications*, 3rd edn, New York, NY: John Wiley & Sons, Wiley-Interscience Publications.
National Audit Office (2001) *A Practical Guide to Sampling*, London: NAO. <www.nao.org.uk/publications/0001/sampling_guide.aspx> [accessed 17 July 2013].

Ethics and risk assessment

Bamberger, M., Rugh, J. and Mabry, L. (2012) 'Ensuring competent and ethical practice in the conduct of the evaluation', chapter 9 in *RealWorld Evaluation: Working under Budget, Time, Data, and Political Constraints*, 2nd edn, Thousand Oaks, CA: Sage Publications.
Bickley, S. (2010) *Safety First: A Safety and Security Handbook for Aid Workers*, London: Save the Children UK. <www.eisf.eu/resources/library/SafetyFirst2010.pdf> [accessed 17 July 2013].
Ellsberg, M. and Heise, L. (2005) *Researching Violence against Women: A Practical Guide for Researchers and Activists*, Washington, DC: World Health Organization, Program for Appropriate Technology in Health (PATH). <www.path.org/publications/files/GBV_rvaw_complete.pdf> [accessed 17 July 2013].
Roche, C. (2010) 'The seeming simplicity of measurement', in Horton, K. and Roche, C. (eds) *Ethical Questions and International NGOs*, Library of Ethics and Applied Philosophy Volume 23, Dordrecht: Springer, pp. 119–46.

Working with children

Save the Children (2005) *Practice Standards in Children's Participation*, London: International Save the Children Alliance, <www.savethechildren.org.uk/resources/online-library/practice-standards-children%E2%80%99s-participation> [accessed 17 July 2013].
UNICEF (2002) *Children Participating in Research, Monitoring and Evaluation (M&E) – Ethics and Your Responsibilities as a Manager*, Evaluation Technical Notes No. 1, New York, NY: UNICEF. <www.unicef.org/evaluation/files/TechNote1_Ethics.pdf> [accessed 17 July 2013].

Statistical analysis

Blaikie, N. (2003) *Analyzing Quantitative Data: From Description to Explanation*, London: Sage Publications.

Deaton, A. (1997) *The Analysis of Household Surveys: A Microeconometric Approach to Development Policy*, Washington, DC, and Baltimore, MD: World Bank and Johns Hopkins University Press.

Osborne, J.W. (2013) *Best Practices in Data Cleaning: A Complete Guide to Everything You Need to Do Before and After Collecting Your Data*, Thousand Oaks, CA: Sage Publications.

Rowntree, D. (1991) *Statistics Without Tears: An Introduction for Non-mathematicians*, London: Penguin Books.

Taylor-Powell, E. (1996) *Analyzing Quantitative Data*, Madison, WI: University of Wisconsin Cooperative Extension Publications. <http://learningstore.uwex.edu/assets/pdfs/g3658-6.pdf> [accessed 17 July 2013].

Qualitative analysis

Gibson, W.J. and Brown, A. (2009) *Working with Qualitative Data*, London: Sage Publications.

Miles, M.B., Huberman, A.M. and Saldaña, J. (2013) *Qualitative Data Analysis: A Methods Sourcebook*, 3rd edn, Thousand Oaks, CA: Sage Publications.

Riley, J. (1996) *Getting the Most from Your Data: A Handbook of Practical Ideas on How to Analyse Qualitative Data*, Bristol: Technical and Educational Services.

Shaw, I.F. (1999) *Qualitative Evaluation*, London: Sage Publications.

Electronic devices

Gibson, J. and McKenzie, D. (2007) 'Using global positioning systems in household surveys for better economics and better policy', *World Bank Research Observer* 22(2): 217–41. <http://elibrary.worldbank.org/content/article/1564-6971-22-2-217-241> [accessed 17 July 2013].

Tomlinson, M., Solomon, W., Singh, Y., Doherty, T., Chopra, M., Ijumba, P., Tsai, A.C. and Jackson, D. (2009) 'The use of mobile phones as a data collection tool: a report from a household survey in South Africa', *BMC Medical Informatics and Decision Making* 9: 51. <http://dx.doi.org/10.1186%2F1472-6947-9-51>.

ANNEX 3

Working with displaced people

The Contribution to Change approach presented in this guide is oriented towards evaluating the recovery of people in situ within their own communities, principally through restoration and/or improvement of their livelihood assets and opportunities. It is not primarily targeted towards the experiences of people living in displacement camps, where the situation of intervention is usually quite different (in its focus on meeting basic needs for a population that is highly dependent on aid).

However, the reality in many disaster situations is that people are displaced from their homes or home sites for varying periods of time – whether they take shelter in others' homes, in public shelters, or in temporary camps. It is important to consider, therefore, how and when the approach may be modified for use with displaced populations. We can consider three options:

- Situations in which some or all people are evacuated but return rapidly to their home sites (i.e. they are displaced for only a short emergency period, e.g. less than four weeks). Here the Contribution to Change approach can proceed as normal because any intervention during displacement will still be in the relief mode. T_{+1} is specified as the time at which the majority of people are in situ.

- Situations in which most people have prolonged displacement before their return (because the home area and/or housing is initially unfit for return, e.g. people are displaced for more than four weeks). Here we need to add an extra step to the Contribution to Change approach because we can assume that intervention during displacement has moved into early recovery mode and in order to assess contribution of interventions in situ we will need to know people's circumstances on their return. So in this case T_{+2} data collection takes place at the time of return (including retrospective data for T_{-1} and T_{+1}) and there is an additional data collection several months later – i.e. at T_{+3}. (Although T_{-1} to T_{+2} to T_{+3} is the main change of interest, in order to understand what has happened we still need to know the status of impacts at T_{+1}.)

- Situations in which people remain very long term in displacement camps and have not returned. Here a recovery process is likely to be observable. However, the role of interventions is likely to be so high in these circumstances that a Contribution to Change approach is unlikely to be warranted, and we suggest that outcomes can probably be captured just as well by more conventional performance-based forms of evaluation.

ANNEX 4

Focusing on intervention beneficiaries

The Contribution to Change approach in this guide has been designed in order to assess recovery and contribution across disaster-affected communities and populations. However, it is also feasible to focus attention more directly on the beneficiaries of specific interventions.

For most of the data collection and analysis steps, this requires minor modification only. A specific household sampling strategy will need to be devised to target intervention beneficiaries, and beneficiary lists can be used to create the sampling frame. Another slight simplification is in how the Contribution to Change statements are derived. In this case, the table for stage B will be as follows.

Stage B: Contribution to recovery achieved

	High	Medium	Low
Stage B: Contribution to recovery achieved **SECTOR** .... **HIGH?** **MEDIUM?** **LOW?**	**The intervention appears to have had a major effect on any positive change experienced in this sector.** The intervention has met the expectation of most (two-thirds or more) of the beneficiaries, and is regarded positively by them. OR There is a general perception and/or evidence that it has had a major effect in bringing about change. OR It is unlikely that the change would have been achieved without the intervention.	**The intervention appears to have made some significant contribution to any positive change achieved in this sector.** The intervention has not fully met the expectations of most (two-thirds or more) of the beneficiaries, but it is regarded as bringing some positive benefit. OR There is a general perception and/or evidence that it has had some clear but limited effect in bringing about change.	**It is unlikely that the intervention has had a positive effect in this sector.** The intervention has not met the expectation of most (two-thirds or more) of the beneficiaries, and is not regarded as bringing a positive benefit. OR There is a general perception and/or evidence that it has not been effective in bringing about change. OR It is likely that the change would have been achieved regardless of the intervention.

Agencies involved

University of East Anglia School of International Development

The School of International Development (DEV), founded in 1973, has a global reputation as a centre for research excellence. DEV applies social and natural resource sciences to the study of economic, social, and environmental change in developing countries. The professional skills, experience, and interests of the School's 30 members of faculty cover both the social and natural sciences: from economics, sociology, gender, and politics, to environmental change, fisheries, soil science, and agronomy. From its foundation, the School has been committed to the interdisciplinary study of development, and it has a strong track record in applied research on disasters and development.

Oxfam

Oxfam is an international confederation of 17 organizations networked together in 94 countries, as part of a global movement for change, to build a future free from the injustice of poverty. Specializing in humanitarian and development work, campaigns and collaboration, the confederation is a global leader in emergency public health work, with a strong focus on providing alternatives to food aid. Please write to any of the 17 member agencies for further information, or visit the website of Oxfam International (the confederation secretariat) at www.oxfam.org for more links.

ECB

The Emergency Capacity Building (ECB) project is a collaborative effort by six agencies: CARE International, Catholic Relief Services, Mercy Corps, Oxfam, Save the Children, and World Vision International. Working with partners, these agencies focus on developing joint initiatives to address issues related to national staff development, disaster risk reduction, accountability to disaster-affected people, and impact measurement. The ECB project aims to improve the speed, quality, and effectiveness of the humanitarian community to save lives, and to improve the welfare and protect the rights of people in emergency situations.